Off the Straight and Narrow

David H Ross

DEDICATION

To my daughter Claire

In recognition of the essential work that Cancer Research UK undertakes to help find cures and ease suffering, 50% of the royalties from the sale of the book will go to this charity.

In aid of

CONTENTS

PREAMBLE

Having reached retirement, time became filled by chilling out with members of my family and involving myself with various volunteer activities, visits to the gym and walks with the local Ramblers group. None of these could be accused of pushing me out of my comfort zone. After a lifetime of pressure and occasional stress from my two careers (logistics management for over thirty years and teaching for the remaining seven years of my working life) I finally admitted to myself that I was actually missing the cut and thrust that these brought. I needed to find something to do that would shake me out of my lethargy; something that I had no apparent aptitude for but would force me to confront this lack of ability head on. Also I wanted to embark on a venture that would involve an extended period of time. This ruled out some of the more extreme ideas that came into (and thankfully quickly departed) my mind. So, no bungee jumping or parachute drops nor putting my hand in a barrel full of spiders; each of which would probably induce a cardiac arrest anyway.

What have I never had any aptitude for? Well, I couldn't embark on a training programme to become the next Casanova as I would need to involve others and wanted to undertake a solo challenge. In my life, had I proof that I had no ability at anything else? I have only ever formally failed at two things, GCE O level English Literature and Religious Studies. Failure in these two subjects was guaranteed because when as a schoolboy I had little or no interest in reading. When I took my O levels you had to be able to give quotes from books and poems. Sitting exams that required such reading meant certain failure if that activity never took place. I hasten to add that since leaving school I have discovered the joy of reading, especially books on History and Science.

Then one night whilst lying awake unable to sleep it came to me - write a book. Obviously, having been involved in business for so long I could write about the dos and don'ts of corporate life. I have come across many characters and incidents that would act as case studies on how to succeed, or not as the case may be. Then again I could write about life as a Chemistry teacher. However, these would still be within my comfort zone. So, what to write about?

If I had not gone down the career paths that I did then I would have wished to be a historian or history teacher. My passion for all things to do with the past stems from Spike Martin, my wonderful History teacher, who made the subject come alive. He taught in the days when teaching was a vocation and he was interested in both the academic and pastoral development of his pupils. At weekends Spike would take a small group of eager boys for walks in the Peak District around Hayfield in Derbyshire. On those hikes he would describe both the geography and the history of the countryside. Perhaps that is where my life-long interest in rambling originates.

As a child, when on a family holiday in North Wales my parents took me into the hills above Conway and left me there (sorry Mum, only kidding). I was most impressed when I came upon a sign that said I was standing on the site of an old Roman road. With great pride I took a stone home with me and told my Dad that it had been laid by a legionary almost two thousand years previously. He suggested that it looked suspiciously like two thousand stones that he had laid previously in the back garden. Many times I have driven down a long straight road and thought, "The Romans built this". (Be honest ... you have had the same thought too.) The A5 north of Birmingham is a case in point. In my naivety I assumed that all long straight roads were built by the Romans and that they only went in for routes without curves. On that basis there must have been many Roman settlements in the

USA as I have driven along some pretty lengthy roads there that you don't need a steering wheel for. Then again, anyone with the nerve to drive along the Hard Knott Pass in the Lake District would realise that the Romans also went in for dangerously precipitous hairpin bends too.

When studying Latin at school, I found the history element more interesting than the language. In fact I can remember very little Latin grammar apart from greeting the teacher with "salve magister" (hello teacher), knowing that agricola meant farmer and being able to translate Caesar's classic line Veni, Vidi, Vici; or as we smutty teenage boys used to say Vidi, Vici, Veni. If you don't know the translation, look it up. Pupils used to be given a newsletter once a month called Acta Diurna (daily acts), but as it was in Latin I only looked at the pictures. However, when we were told about the adventures of the Roman legions I was spellbound. Who couldn't be gripped by the travails of the Ninth Legion? This was an elite army that saw service in many areas of the Roman Empire before being sent to Britain. The Legion was sent north to York where they built the stronghold of Eburacum. Many of the soldiers were killed in battle with Queen Boudicca's Iceni. And then, nothing. The whole Legion disappears. Were they wiped out by the Picts or just disbanded? We don't know. Whilst we are on the subject of Boudicca, how come she changed her name from Boadicea? That was her name when I was taught at school. Then again, I have found some books that spell her name Boudica and Buduica.

When in Rome I was awed by the ancient monuments (and the more recent Victor Emmanuel II building, which seems at first out of place but then grows on you due to its sheer majesty). I also marvelled at the ability of a relatively small conurbation's ability to expand and control the Empire without the benefit of modern communication networks (both physical and ethereal). Not only did it cover vast distances but also lasted many years; the western

Empire for around just over 500 years and the Eastern one for a further 1000 years in one form or another. In Britain alone the Empire lasted for 400 years. Rome also became the seat of one of the major religions on the planet, Christianity. To help with communications the Romans used the network of rivers running through the Empire; for example the Loire and Seine in France, the Rhine in Germany and Danube across Eastern Europe (the latter two acting as both means of transport and boundaries). As well as these natural waterways the Romans built great water transport systems, the aqueducts. In addition they constructed a series of roads across the Empire that would make transport, communication and control easier. The first of these was built around 300BC, over three centuries before the Romans arrived in Britain. So by the time of their arrival on these shores, the building and maintenance of their roads was well established, as was their use in expanding and maintaining the Empire.

The content of my book was now obvious; take a road trip along the old Roman roads that used to crisscross this island, describing my journey in terms of what I encountered and learned along the way both in terms of Roman and more recent history (and maybe throw in a bit of personal history too). This would certainly take longer than confronting my arachnophobia or fear of heights. Having none but a romantic notion of any of the roads that the Romans built in England (not forgetting Scotland and Wales too) I realised that before my trip started I would have to spend many hours researching so that I could both decide on which Roman roads to follow and which historical curios to write about. Also, should I go dressed as a Roman legionary, carrying all my provisions and pitching my tent each night after a long and sweaty foot slog? Or, perhaps as a Roman commander who used the transport of the day and had his accommodation made ready for him. No brainer! Yes, I would be walking most of my route. However, I accept that motorways and major trunk routes have been built on top of some Roman roads with no alternative paths or lanes. It would be unsafe for a lone walker to attempt these. Intrepid I may be, but foolhardy no. In those circumstances I would occasionally have to rely on public transport, but this would be the exception. As to accommodation, I would try to stay in places that were not part of national chains.

1 WHERE TO BEGIN?

"I need some books about the Roman roads in Britain", I said to the librarian.

She looked up from her computer with an expression that suggested that I was her first nerd of the day.

"We've got a good one on Hadrian's Wall", she enthused.

"No good", I replied. "It is roads not walls that I'm interested in".

"Tullie House Museum in Carlisle is very good if you want to know about the history of the Romans in the area", she continued helpfully. "They've got a mock-up of part of Hadrian's Wall, or is it a World War One trench? No, definitely the wall. They are very strong on the Border Reivers too, but they came after the Romans I think".

"Sorry, it is Roman roads I'm looking for".

"Ah, I remember driving on one just north of Birmingham. Long and straight it was. Quite boring actually". She paused for breath and then continued, "I remember my husband said that it must be a Roman road because it was so straight." Then with an afterthought she added, "And flat. Flat, long, straight and boring".

Now I'm not very good at steering people in my direction so I heard myself say, "Yes, it is the A5, I think. I remember driving on it and thinking exactly the same as your husband. I was driving to North Wales for a camping holiday in Snowdonia. They don't have straight, flat, boring roads there".

"Or in Cumbria," she said, bringing the conversation back to her home area. "Strange that, as the Romans had a big presence up here. Did I tell you that we have a great book about Hadrian's Wall?"

I reminded her that it was Roman roads that I was interested in.

In an attempt to demonstrate her willingness to be helpful, the librarian continued, "Well, they must have built a road alongside the wall so the soldiers could get from Carlisle to Newcastle easily and also to transfer all the bricks for the wall".

"You must be right there" I considered. "They would have needed a service road for all the provisions too. And perhaps service areas every few miles, filling stations for the chariots".

Either not recognising or ignoring my futile attempt at humour, she added thoughtfully, "It probably wasn't called Carlisle in those days, or Newcastle. Shall I look up on the internet what they used to call Newcastle?"

I needed to get back on track so nipped in whilst she was taking a breath, "But do you have any books on Roman roads?" Too late!

"So you want to know what the Romans called Newcastle then? Probably something like Newcastlium, like Londinium was their name for London. Let's see what the computer says", the librarian said. Whilst waiting for the information to load up she added helpfully, "Wonder how the Romans managed without computers. They did ever so well, what with conquering the known world without computers or phones and things. And they say the Romans brought civilisation to England". She stared intently at the screen, eager to expand her and my knowledge. "Aha! Pons Aelius. Well that's weird. At Least Londinium looks like London. Let's just check Carlisle for you".

For me!

"Here it comes, Luguvallium! They're having a laugh now, that's the name of a tranquiliser and I didn't know the Romans invented them. No wonder the Roman Empire fell if the soldiers kept popping pills."

I was beginning to pine for my comfort zone. So far my researches had apparently established that their roads are long, straight, flat and boring and also that the Romans may have invented tranquilisers. Oh, and that the library had a very good book about Hadrian's Wall.

"Anything else I can help you with?"

"Just one more thing, please. Do you have any books on Roman roads in Britain?" I asked sheepishly.

"Right, let's see". Once the computer had been galvanised back into life the librarian was actually a veritable font of knowledge and she agreed to get a number of books sent to the library for me to delve through. She pointed out that some were reference books only so that I could not take them away with me. However, she would find a quiet corner somewhere for me to have a read. I assumed all corners were quiet in libraries. She said that I was allowed to take out twenty non-fiction books at any one time.

"Crickey, I better bring a wheelbarrow next time," I said.

"Ah, I don't think wheelbarrows are allowed in the library," she added in a matter of fact way. "Oh, before you go. If you don't mind me asking, what do you need the books for?"

"I was thinking of building a Roman road out of them, ha-ha."

"If you don't want to tell me then that's okay" she uttered.

"Sorry, my attempt at humour again. I am going to follow the route of a Roman road."

She considered this and then advised me, "I don't think that there are any left in this country. I mean, both Romans and Roman roads".

"I know", I clarified, "I will be following as close to the original route as is now possible".

Ever helpful the librarian said, "There is a lovely Italian restaurant just around the corner from the library. And a Domino's Pizza place. They are both Roman, I think".

I got up to go.

She said, "Good luck. I will phone you when the books arrive."

I thanked the librarian and departed. As I left I noticed her turning to a colleague and mouth something that looked like "weirdo". On the way home I bought a Dictaphone. Somewhere in my mind I felt that this would be an essential tool in my quest. At home I conducted essential research with my Dictaphone. Having put it in the corner of the living room, I switched it on and started walking around reciting nursery rhymes, alternating between whispering and shouting. A couple of minutes later, out of the corner of my eye I spotted my postman staring at the window. He mouthed a two syllable word beginning with W but I don't think it was weirdo.

With my soon to arrive books and trusty Dictaphone I would be ready to plan my grand adventure.

***

Coming to these shores would have been a grand adventure for the Romans too. In fact, they must have enjoyed the experience so much that they didn't invade once but three times.

Most of us will probably know what happened in 1066. That was the year that William of Normandy landed in England, promptly fell flat on his face on the beach, wiped himself down and then proceeded to conquer much of England and Wales. As his invasion succeeded William seems to have changed his surname from "of Normandy" to "the Conqueror".

However, ask people what happened in 55BC (and again in 54BC) and you will start to get some blank expressions. Mention AD43 and the chances are that very few people will be able to say what momentous event occurred.

In 55BC, Julius Caesar (he of "et tu Brute", Ides of March etc. fame) mounted an expedition to the shores of what eventually became known as Kent. Two ill equipped legions made the crossing in rather unfavourable weather conditions. Their cavalry support was unable to land due to this. Lack of suitable provisions and kit suggest that the expedition was not planned as an invasion, more a "dipping the toe in the water" affair. As it was late in the campaigning season, the weather was also against maintaining supplies from Gaul (modern day France). Within a short space of time and no battles of any note, Caesar returned to Gaul. His spin doctors worked the oracle well and his brief sojourn was viewed as an achievement warranting hearty celebrations in Rome. In his play "Julius Caesar", Shakespeare does not quote Caesar saying to the senate, "Well, I had a couple of months to spare so popped over the old briny to Blighty, stirred things up a bit, showed them that we were not to be messed with and then popped back to Gaul. Foray fine, weather awful. Looking forward to spending summer there next year".

The following year, in 54BC, Caesar invaded in Kent with a far larger and better prepared force of at least four legions plus cavalry support. This had the look of an army that was prepared to linger longer. As it was earlier in the year, weather conditions were more favourable too. Progress was made inland as far as the Thames and Caesar's main protagonist, Cassivellaunus, resorted to guerrilla tactics rather than pitched battle to hound the invader. Infighting and betrayal amongst the local tribes resulted in Cassivellaunus surrendering and vowing not to wage war against the Romans. However, growing unrest in Gaul meant that Caesar could not pursue his invasion indefinitely. Hostages and tribute were agreed and then Caesar returned to Gaul. The Romans had only got as far as Kent and the Thames valley. Again, in a historical context, this could not be regarded as a successful invasion by the Romans. They had no impact on the cultural life of the Island and no lasting Roman structures nor administrative methods can be attributed to these incursions. On his departure from the island, Caesar took all Roman troops with him back to Gaul.

At the time of Caesar's visits, communications on the mainland were somewhat rudimentary with poorly maintained trackways (like the Icknield Way) and rivers (Severn, Trent) being the main routes. A mishmash of tribal alliances, some working with and some against the Romans after they departed, meant that there was no unifying force that would bring sufficient stability to form a common island interest in terms of security and communication. Conditions were ripe for invasion once the Romans were confident that they had stability in Gaul. And so we get to the third and final and extremely successful Roman invasion of Britain.

Don't get me wrong, I have nothing against Julius Caesar. After all, until his bad day at the office on 15th March 43BC, he controlled a mighty Empire. Shakespeare wrote a play about him and many famous actors have sought to portray him on stage and screen (including John Gielgud, Rex Harrison and Kenneth Williams). However, I am always wary of someone who has a great PR team. He returned a hero after two abortive invasions of Britain for goodness sake. Even Caesar himself could not resist glorifying himself in his series of books on the Gallic Wars.

Bit of trivia: John Wilkes Booth, assassin of Abraham Lincoln, played Mark Anthony in a stage version of Julius Caesar.

Unlike the glorification of Caesar, the Roman emperor who oversaw the successful invasion of Britain in AD43 (that lead to

400 years of Roman rule, don't forget) has gone down in history as a stammering cripple. Claudius, due to his infirmity, was never going to make a dashing general, leading his troops to victory. His strengths lay in his administrative skills. He also ensured that many new roads and aqueducts were built throughout the Empire. The general that he chose to lead the invasion of Britain (and become its first Roman governor) was Aulus Plautius, relative of Claudius's first wife. The invasion almost didn't take place. The Roman troops were reluctant to board the ships and risk their lives on the tidal sea. For many this would have been their first experience of the power of the tides. Allegedly, an ex-Greek slave, Narcissus who was one of Claudius' advisers, is supposed to have persuaded the legionaries to do what Plautius and his officers could not.

In the run up to the invasion there had been strong cultural, diplomatic and economic links building between the southeast of the island and Rome. Tribal infighting again weakened the Island's ability to defend itself. Two big tribes in the area were the Atrebates (allied to Rome) and the Catuvellauni (who had deposed king Verica, the king of the Atrebates). At the time of the invasion the Atrebates joined forces with the Romans. There was nothing unusual about this. Roman conquests relied on alliances and use of allies in helping to supress opposition. Then Rome and its allies would share the spoils of war. Having got as far as the Thames, Plautius waited for the arrival of Claudius before advancing on the Catuvellauni capital, Camulodunum (modern day Colchester). A Roman province was set up and, again typical of the Roman method of conquest, alliances were agreed with surrounding tribes. Thus a strong foothold was established in Britain which allowed for the gradual expansion of the Roman Empire north and westwards.

So, why did the Romans bother? It was not about securing their border. The English Channel was as good a frontier as one could get. Perhaps it was in part to get access to the mineral wealth of Britannia, although the rulers of Rome were already extremely rich and mainland Europe was still a wealth generator. Maybe Claudius was looking for a glorious campaign victory to secure his position as emperor. This seems like a reasonable suggestion, especially in the light of the fact that Plautius waited for the arrival of Claudius (and a herd of elephants) before his final push against Camulodunum. Do you remember how the Falklands War in the late 20th century enhanced Margaret Thatcher's reputation as a no nonsense prime minister?

Another explanation, less plausible in my opinion, involved the arrival of Verica at the court of Claudius. Verica (also known as Bericus), as mentioned above, had been deposed as king of the Atrebates by Caratacus, king of the Catuvellauni. The Atrebates had been loyal supporters of Rome since the invasion of Julius Caesar and Verica hoped that a Roman army would be despatched to reinstate him. From a PR point of view, this would seem a far nobler reason to invade Britain rather than self-glorification. Many nations since this period have used alleged support of the oppressed as a reason for invasion and subjugation. Patricia Southern in "Roman Britain, A New History 55BC-AD450" (page 54), sums up things perfectly,

> "He [Verica] *perhaps did not anticipate that the response to his request for help would result in the Roman occupation of Britain for nearly four hundred years."*

Whatever the reason for arriving, by AD84 the conquest of England, Wales and Scotland south of a line from Glasgow to Edinburgh was complete and relatively secure, with a further push up to the Moray Firth in the final year. However, in AD185 the Scottish territory north of Hadrian's Wall was abandoned.

During those forty years of expansion the most famous rebellion against Roman rule was in AD60-61. Boudicca (she of the changed name), queen of the Iceni tribe, led a revolt that almost succeeded. The part of the Ninth Legion that was not wiped out took bloody revenge once the revolution had been supressed.

To consolidate the territory gained, the Romans built a series of forts to house and safeguard troops. These forts were of different size and use. A castrum, for example, was a fortified military camp (look for town names with …chester in) that was a major site for holding troops that could combat insurrection or protect the surroundings. Many small auxiliary forts were built, more as barracks and stores rather than somewhere that could withstand a sustained attack. Around the forts communities formed, earning their living supplying the day to day needs of the soldiers and also the luxuries and trinkets that a soldier's pay could buy. These communities were in addition to towns and villages already established prior to the Roman invasion. It should be noted that less than thirty new Roman towns developed in Britain. It was here that the British elite took on Roman ways and helped maintain the Roman administration of the conquered territory. In return for their loyalty they were well rewarded. Much of the folk in the rest of Britain got on with their day to day struggles and tolerated Roman rule rather than take on its way of life and language. For this reason we do not see the widespread use of the Latin language and Roman place-names.

Essential elements of the Roman subjugation and consolidation of their Empire in Britain were not only a strong military presence but also an efficient civil service, production of a loyal ruling class of Britons and a reliable communication network. What was of lesser importance was the building of aqueducts. Some were created to help with the mining activities (a huge source of revenue for the Empire). Baths were less important than in other parts of the Empire. I am not suggesting that the average Briton was a smelly, uncivilised lout compared to the Romans. Perhaps the British climate reduced the need for regular bathing rather than the inhabitants being less interested in their personal hygiene than their continental counterparts. The ability for the weather to water crops and supply regular drinking water also reduced the requirement for aqueducts.

***

And now we get to the Roman roads. The more I delved into my subject the more engrossed I became. Those of you who have seen that excellent television series fronted by Michael Portillo, called Great British Railway Journeys, will remember that he always had to hand a copy of George Bradshaw's Victorian Railway Guidebook. My "bible" became Ivan D. Margary's "Roman Roads in Britain", 1973 edition.

Anyone who undertakes a study of British Roman roads should have this seminal tome at the ready. Margary had an obvious deep love of the subject and I understand that he was always willing to give assistance to interested parties. He catalogued roads and routes, major and minor, and gave them reference numbers. Where applicable, I will refer to Margary's road numbering system for the sake of consistency. He also indicated distances between the various sections of Roman roads. Basically, Margary is my Bradshaw. I was lucky enough to purchase a copy via eBay as it has long been out of print. Another must-read is M.C. Bishop's "The Secret History of the Roman Roads of Britain". He delves into the whys and wherefores of the subject in a logical manner. Another work of mention is "An Atlas of Roman Britain" by Barri Jones and David Mattingly; lots of maps and diagrams. My favourite book, however, is "Roman Britain, A New History 55BC-AD450" by Patricia Southern. It covers the subject in great detail and reads like an adventure story too. It is a real page-turner.

But which Roman road should I follow? Logically, I would start my journey as did the Romans, somewhere on the Kent coast, then head for London. Next, I would take Ermine Street (after a brief detour to follow Claudius' march on Colchester) following the route of the Ninth Legion (the one that disappeared from history), and finish in York. I had a plan germinating!

But where to start exactly? Probably the invasion force was split into three and landed close to Lympne (Roman name Lemanis), Dover (Dubris) and Richborough (Rutupiae) on the coast of Kent. I say probably because the archaeological evidence is not detailed enough to create certainty. Cassius Dio, writing in the 3rd century, tantalisingly talks about three waves. But was this in three different places? Patricia Southern (page 67), says,

> *"Richborough was later used as one of the main entry points to Britain, and a huge arch was built, foursquare, massive and designed to impress."*

Aulus Plautius, the leader of the whole force, is thought to have led the invasion at Richborough and that the Ninth Legion was part of that landing. And that is good enough for me. So, goodbye Penrith, hello Richborough.

2 RICHBOROUGH TO CANTERBURY

Route: Margary 10, "Roman Roads in Britain" (pages 36-39).

With great enthusiasm I packed my new extra-large rucksack. With somewhat less enthusiasm I just about managed to pick it up and pull the straps across my shoulders. This I hadn't bargained for. Whilst trudging the mile from my house to Penrith station I wondered how I would cope for the rest of my trip (I have suffered on and off with a bad back and have an arthritic hip – my Mum sympathetically informed me recently that it was old age creeping up on me). By the time I arrived at the station my neck was feeling the strain so I was glad that it was time for the train to take the strain.

It was packed and I was grateful that I had booked a seat reservation. From Penrith down to Warrington I was privileged to see the best game of train chess that I have ever witnessed. For the uninitiated this involves getting on a train without a seat reservation and seeing how many times you get asked to move. A couple confidently positioned themselves at a table seat. At Oxenholme they were asked to move. They had to split up and were now seated at opposite ends of the carriage. On departure from Lancaster they both had to move again. The man sat next to me. The same process was repeated at Preston and Wigan. On departure from Warrington they had one final move to make (next stop was London) and this was the train chess equivalent of check mate. The table seats that they had started from had become vacant so they moved back there triumphantly.

It took me the best part of the day to get from my home in Cumbria to the town of Sandwich in Kent for an overnight stop in a hotel. Part of the way down I kept awake long enough to view the section of the rail journey where four modes of transport from different ages run parallel with each other. This was Watford Gap, confusingly named as it has nothing to do with the town of Watford. However, the motorway services on the M1 are named after it. Watford Gap is a geological feature that has a gap in the landscape which has been used for various forms of transport; railway, motorway, canal and Roman road. The train was doing over 100 mph. The southbound traffic on the motorway was doing about the same speed as I would be walking at later.

Sandwich is one of the Cinque Ports and home to the Royal St George's golf club. The original Cinque Ports (Dover, Hastings, Hythe, New Romney and Sandwich) were maritime towns that, by Royal Charter in 1155, had to make available ships for the protection of the realm. In return, each town was free from taxes and import duties and had degrees of autonomy that other towns did not enjoy. They became smugglers paradises.

When I arrived in Sandwich it was dark but not threatening. One other passenger got off, a lady in her early twenties. I walked a couple of paces behind her and listened in on her phone conversation. At the point that she said, "Well if you f***ing think that I am f***ing coming all the way to Blackpool just to give you a couple of fixes you have got another f***ing thing coming", I slowed my pace and increased the distance between us. What sort of place had I come to? It had suddenly become very threatening. Was this the drugs capital of Kent? I need not have worried. Soon I entered a series of quaint streets and eventually reached the Kings Arms, my stop for the night.

I peered through the window. It looked cosy and inviting and the open hearth wood burning fire was beckoning me. However, I couldn't find the way in. Three times I passed by the window with the roaring fire. People in the pub started to look at me and laugh.

This did not bode well for my road trip. If I was unable to find my way into a pub what chance of navigating over three hundred miles to York? On my fourth circuit I caught sight of a now clearly obvious sign that said "Entry this way". Having booked in I had intended to wander through the town to get a meal and then an early night. However, the hotel staff and the fire were so welcoming that I decided to have my meal there. Food and beer (notice I did not say ale. Why not will be explained when I get to Faversham) were excellent. I particularly recommend the button mushrooms in a bacon, cream and garlic sauce. I did not have as early night as planned. If this was a foretaste of my future overnight stops then I had much to look forward to.

Next morning it was gloriously sunny so I sauntered around Sandwich before breakfast. It was a very pleasant place with the river Stour lazily snaking its way through the still sleeping town. After a hearty breakfast I filled my flask and having bought a picnic lunch whilst on my pre-breakfast stroll, I set off with the wonderful late autumnal clear blue sky above. The sun was still low in the sky when I arrived at Richborough fort.

When you arrive there the first thing that strikes you is, "Where is the sea?" I was going to start from the initial point of entry into Britain and walk along the first known Roman road from Richborough to Ash and then on to Canterbury. But hang on a minute, there is a bit missing from Richborough to the sea! Over two miles in fact. How come the Romans forgot to build that bit?

I needed to realise that 2000 years ago the topography of Britain was somewhat different. Wide, difficult to cross rivers could have silted up and conversely, streams may have become raging rivers that would now be difficult to ford. Where we see rolling countryside there may have been dense forests. More importantly, with regards to my start point, the coastline and low lying areas of the Southeast were substantially different to what we see today. The Isle of Thanet was truly an island. So, could Richborough have been accessible from the English Channel? Tony Wilmott, senior archaeologist with English Heritage, reporting in 2008 from an archaeological dig, said that whilst digging in a trench alongside the Roman wall his team had eventually reached what he realised was the Roman beach. They had uncovered the old harbour alongside the wall of the fortress.

All that is left of the maritime connection is the river Stour on the fort's doorstep. The river meanders crazily from the North Sea, at first south to Sandwich and then in a generally westerly direction (past the Stodmarsh National Nature Reserve and through Canterbury), traverses the Kent Downs on its way southward (via Ashford), and then turns northwest and north before finally running out of steam at Lenham. Not a straight section in sight. If you are wondering why uplands are called Downs (and sand dunes are small sand hills) then it is probably because the word down is based on the Old English word dun, meaning hill.

Richborough fort is an English Heritage site. I have the greatest respect for the likes of English Heritage and the National Trust.

For annual membership fees of £46 and £65 respectively (2017 rates), I have unlimited access to their sites and car parks. Both do immense work to endeavour to not only preserve our antiquities and countryside but also to ensure that the public can have reasonable access. I am yet to meet an employee of either at their sites who is not helpful and enthusiastic.

Although there is not much left of the fort, you can still get an appreciation of its previous grandeur and size. The site was such a pivotal part of the Roman occupation of Britain that a triumphal arch was built here. You can imagine people passing through being told, "This way for Britain et la bas pour Gaul. Get your triumphal arch mementos here. Best local oysters in the Empire." In fact, there is not much left in the surrounding area to suggest that this was once a thriving town that rivalled Dover for importance. All around was flat, open farmland with only the giant buildings of modern industry intruding on the horizon a few miles north-eastwards.

Make no mistake though, this was a crucial location as far as the Roman Empire was concerned. They eventually constructed one of their Saxon Shore fortresses here. The Saxon Shore forts were built along both sides of the English Channel in the third century AD to help reduce the impact of marauding pirates and tribes based in modern day Germany (Angles, Saxons, Franks and Jutes). The Roman Empire never successfully penetrated east of the Rhine so it became a hot bed of restlessness with people seeking to make incursions into the revenue rich lands of the Empire. During my hiking through Kent I would cross the long distance path, the Saxon Shore Way, a number of times.

Whereas Richborough was abandoned as a military establishment when the Romans left Britain, it did have two war related uses in later imperial conflicts. Firstly it was used in World War 1. Derek Lord stated in 2003,

1.   "During the First World War 1914/18 a secret "Q" port by the banks of the River Stour was the starting point of a ferry service for troops and munitions to France and Flanders. Camps were occupied by thousands of soldiers who were taken by day or by night across the North Sea and the Channel to Dunkirk and Calais.

2.   The chosen spot for the hidden port was under the Roman fortress of Richborough; and a railway was constructed from the main line which passes under the Saxon walls to the banks of the Stour. The river mouth was dredged; and a new port of embarkation was created. The camp was constructed in the marshlands on both sides of the river.

3.   Most of the work undertaken by the Royal Engineers and much of the equipment and arms for the Ypres Salient were sent across from Richborough Port, using sea going barges and the very first roll-on roll-off ferries."

Then a further use was found for Richborough in the Second World War. Again Derek Lord says,

"For nearly twenty years the Richborough Camp was not used until the end of the year 1938, when Sandwich received more than 5000 Jewish and political refugees from Germany, Austria and Czechoslovakia, driven out by Nazi persecution ... At the end of August, 1939, Britain was at war with Germany and a large majority of the men in the camp volunteered and eventually were accepted for service in and attached to the British forces ... In 1942 Richborough Camp became a post of the Marines, named H.M.S. Robertson: and the former Q port was again a hive of industry. Part of the Mulberry harbour to be towed to the Normandy coast, for "D Day" attack on the German wall, was built there by the Royal Engineers."

Before setting off from Richborough to Canterbury (Roman name Durovernum) I had my club sandwich and a cuppa whilst looking towards Sandwich and its famous golf club.

**

I was now tracing the footsteps of the Roman invasion force, keeping as close as possible to the original Roman road. But how long did it take to build a campaign route or metalled Roman road? We have no documentary evidence to categorically answer this. There was already a well-established system of tracks and ridgeways in many parts of Britain. The Roman methodology involved advancing along the best possible routes (which could have included going along existing tracks), forging rudimentary campaign tracks and then leaving teams of surveyors, engineers and navvies behind to construct metalled roads. Thus the advancing army would then have both a means of communication and supply lines to the rear. Roman cavalry would not have used the metalled surfaces as their horses were unshod and were better suited to travelling alongside the roads.

As to how long did it take to construct the roads we can only come up with a best guess? In 1865 in the American Civil War, during General Sherman's march through the Carolinas his army was able to construct roads at the rate of ten miles per day. Their method involved cutting down trees and laying a wooded track called a corduroy road. A similar prehistoric track has been unearthed in the Somerset levels. John Peddie has calculated that using 1,000 Royal Engineers they could construct an assault road at the rate of one yard per man per day. In the 1700's, during the subjugation of the Highlands of Scotland, proper military roads were constructed at the rate of between 1.5 and 2 yards per man per day. So, for the Romans, it really depends on how many people were allocated to the road building and whether the road was a campaign route or more robust metalled road. What is definite is that the Roman army did not delay its advance until a metalled road had been constructed.

***

Suitably refreshed, I followed Cooper Street Drove and minor footpaths (the route of the Roman road out of Richborough) and reached Ash. It was hard to imagine that part of the 40,000 strong army had walked along here in AD43. Sadly, to my eyes it is not obvious that a Roman road did pass this way. Then again there are few sections of any of the Roman roads that can be easily recognised nowadays. The road would usually have been built on an embankment called an agger. The material for the agger would come from either side of the proposed road. A typical road would be built in three layers to a total depth of about one metre; large stones and sand at the bottom with a layer of pebbles and gravel on top and topped off by paving stones. The roads were up to 8 metres wide with drainage ditches running alongside. I occasionally did see evidence of the aggers and their drainage ditches as these are construction methods often used for modern roads.

From Ash I made my way eastwards to Canterbury, following as close as possible to the original route of the Roman road. Less than two miles out of Ash I paid a visit to Wingham Wildlife Park. For its size it houses a remarkable number and variety of species. Opening in 1986, it has steadily developed into a well organised and visitor friendly attraction. The top lake has an island that is home to a family of Mandrills. I really appreciate it when an enclosure is designed without cages or windows. The lake acts as a natural barrier. The mandrills were introduced in 2012 as part of the European Endangered Species Programme (EESP). When I first read about this I thought to myself "Hang on a tick, mandrills are not Europeans". On further investigation I found out that the EESP co-ordinates the activities of European zoos and aquaria in their work on endangered species from around the World.

Lesson on Latin plurals: aquarium and aquaria, stadium and stadia, medium and media. So, if we have a vase full of geraniums should we say we have a vase of gerania? And if we have a load of the bacterium (plural bacteria) called genitalium should they be called genitalia?

Whilst wandering around the hamlet of Wingham I noticed that there was an infrequent bus service to the tiny village of Plucks Gutter which houses a hostelry called The Dog and Duck in Plucks Gutter. I'm not making this up. Imagine being stopped by the Police after one over the eight and then asked where you have been? The village is sited at the confluence of the Great Stour (the one that meanders crazily) and the Little Stour. Sadly, I did not have time to visit this tongue twister of an inn.

Stopping for a baguette and a beer in Wingham, I surreptitiously shared the sausage filling with the pub's dog. I wasn't noticed and I don't think the dog let on either. After lunch I decided to go slightly off the straight and narrow route of the Roman road and followed a perfectly straight path across corn fields to Ickham. The fields through which the path crossed had been ploughed up but kindly farmers had run tractors or quad bikes along the route of the path so I had no problem following it. In Ickham I got my first view of the iconic oast houses of Kent (see below). These are now mainly converted into housing and are no longer used to dry the hops for the brewing industry.

After around twelve miles of trekking with a heavy pack I was extremely sore and tired. I just about managed to walk up the hill to my hotel, the Evenhill in Littlebourne, checked in, went to my room, made a coffee, ate the biscuits and went to sleep. Not even the Tuesday night special steak rate in the hotel restaurant could entice me from my bed.

Previously the manor of Littlebourne was part of the estate owned by St Augustine's abbey in Canterbury for which it apparently provided grapes. The parish church, dating from the 13th century is dedicated to St. Vincent (patron saint of winemakers). So the idea that the parish did grow vines is not that far-fetched. The church is well worth a visit. I particularly appreciated the stained glass windows, designed by 19th century artist Nathaniel Westlake. There were two huge, what I assumed to be, yew trees in the graveyard and a line of rose bushes, some still in bloom, leading from the lychgate to the church entrance. Very pretty.

Next morning I walked a couple of hundred yards out of Littlebourne and investigated Pine Wood, which you come to just past Evenhill Road on the right. The main Ash to Canterbury road takes a gentle southerly curve around Pine Wood. Just as the curve shifts north-westerly there is a track going southwest (and in the opposite direction, northeast through the wood). Halfway through the wood it becomes a very clear path that then leaves the wood along the line of a hedgerow and eventually meets Court Hill. This track is part of a minor Roman road. The main Roman road from Richborough to Canterbury goes through Pine Wood. Look on Google Maps (satellite view) and you will see traces of the tracks in the wood. Remains of an agger were visible when the wood was clear. Sadly, I found no such traces. What Margery would have given for Google Maps! There is a program on TV called the Flying Archaeologist. It is very informative but the BBC could have saved some of my licence money if they had used Google Maps instead of paying for an aeroplane and pilot. They could have called the programme the Google-eyed Archaeologist.

I wanted to make time for a slight detour of about half a mile to walk down to Howletts Wild Animal Park. What with Wingham Wildlife Park, I had the chance to visit two well stocked zoos within three miles of each other. I seemed to remember the name Howletts. Then it came to me, John Aspinall. He set up a private zoo in 1957 (following a large win at the races) that has become renowned, especially for its troupe of western lowland gorillas. The zoo also featured in a children's TV series called Roar, first broadcast in the late 1990's. Aspinall was also a close friend of Lord Lucan (he who disappeared after the brutal slaying of the family nanny) and it was alleged at the time that Aspinall helped Lucan escape. This was never proven. Aspinall maintained that Lucan had done the decent thing and killed himself. Well, he would say that wouldn't he? Another rumour told to me by Lesley, one of my sisters, was that Lucan's body was fed to the lions at the zoo. Then again this is the sister that said that one new year she would celebrate Mahogany in Scotland. Tragedy has also struck at Howletts zoo. In 1980 Aspinall had to shoot a tiger that had killed two keepers. In 1994 the head keeper was killed by another tiger.

As it was late in the season I had the zoo almost to myself. Whilst looking at an enclosure with a mother and baby rhino, a lady with a clipboard strolled up and appeared to count the rhinos and make a note. She went to the next enclosure and repeated the process – one rhino adult female, one rhino baby male. Had the zoo expected a rhino to have escaped during the night or perhaps another one to have smuggled its way in? Curiosity got the better of me so I asked her what she was doing. Apparently she was checking to see how far the babies were walking away from their mothers. To the untrained eye, they seemed to be sticking close to mummy.

Talking of babies, the proudest moment of my life was when I held my daughter for the first time. From my point of view the birth was relatively easy; I just had to sit and make encouraging noises every so often. My ex-wife, Marion, may possibly have other memories of the occasion. I once asked my sister Isabel to describe labour. She told me to stuff a melon up each nostril at the same time and I would get the picture. Claire was only a few minutes old and compared to me was tiny. Then again she was tiny, weighing in at 6 pounds 4 ounces (that is 2.8 kilograms for those of you reading sur le continent). How come, after converting to kilos from pounds ages ago, people in this country still quote baby birth weight in pounds and ounces? All these years later and Claire continues to produce proud moments for her doting Dad, and in return he still manages to embarrass her.

Anyway, this old gorilla made his way to the "Old Gorillas" enclosure and spent ages in total awe of them. They looked so powerful yet gentle. The silverback came over to check me out and we eyeballed each other for a couple of minutes. He then grunted and flicked a giant medicine ball about twenty yards just to remind me who was boss in this part of the zoo. I felt that taking any pictures of these wonderful creatures would have been an insult to their dignity.

Back to the route of the Roman road and onwards to Canterbury. On the left before reaching the city I passed St Martin's Hospital. For those wishing to pitch a tent, there is the Canterbury Club campsite next to the hospital.

***

I have no desire to set foot or any other part of my anatomy in a tent ever again. The last two times I have camped I can honestly say that it could have gone better. For the penultimate experience I unknowingly completed the Yorkshire three peaks challenge (Pen Y Ghent, Whernside and Ingleborough) in just under twelve hours. I had been invited for what I assumed to be a stroll by my then best friend, a work colleague called Dave Mason. Unaware of what I was undertaking I turned up in training shoes and t shirt. We started at the quaint town of Horton- in-Ribblesdale. It was a lovely, sunny day and I felt at one with the beautiful outdoors.

Dave pointed at a nearby peak and said, "Pen Y Ghent, over 2,200 feet. Do it in two hours."

I was shocked. "But I'm not equipped for that, Dave," I said. However, I persevered and reached the summit with an air of deep satisfaction. I felt great and was looking forward to getting back to Horton for a few beers. I still loved the great outdoors.

Dave pointed in the distance and said to my disbelief, "Right, that's one ticked off. Next its Whernside, 2,400ft, only five miles away."

"Bloody hell, Dave. Are you serious?" I exclaimed. But he was off already. I followed behind muttering to myself. We crossed a lengthy peat bog that I only sank in up to my shins. Next we passed under a rather impressive railway viaduct that I later found out was the famous Ribblehead viaduct. It was a long hard slog up the side of Whernside but we made it to the top. I was knackered but reluctantly admitted that the views in all directions were amazing; I could even see Morecambe Bay in the distance. Hopefully we would get down this peak and catch a bus back to Horton. I had had enough of the great outdoors.

What happened next can only be described as a bad dream. Dave pointed westward and said, "Last one, Ingleborough, 2,300ft".

"You must be bloody kidding Dave. I can hardly stand."

"It's on the way back," Dave said in what he thought was his motivational voice. "There is a pub on the way that we can pop in to for a quick pint".

That was all the motivation I needed. My feet were red raw but my thirst needed quenching and then I would be ready for the final ascent. The pub was closed. I reckon that idiot ex-friend Mason knew this all along. Somehow I managed to crawl my way up Ingleborough and was faced with the most incredible limestone pavements I had ever seen. I was back in love with the great outdoors.

"Just five miles easy walk back now," said Dave enthusiastically. And I did it. I must have been on autopilot as I have no recollection of getting back to Horton.

"Twenty three miles in twelve hours. We met the challenge!" said Dave triumphantly. I just needed a long soak in a bath but we still had to sort our B and B out.

Dave smiled and said, "Right, I'll get the tent out of the car then. You can pitch it whilst I get some food for us".

I'm afraid I then used the F word.

The last time I spent the night in a tent (notice that I did not say slept in a tent) was with that lunatic Mason. We had planned a weekend walking and camping in Snowdonia. I had come prepared this time. After a gruelling, but most enjoyable day's hiking we pitched our tent in a field.

"Where are the showers, Dave?" I asked.

"There are none here."

"What about toilets then?"

"Use the bush at the end of the field," Dave replied, adding helpfully, "Here's some toilet paper."

I spent the night constantly rolling down the tent (funny that, must be hills in Snowdonia). A meeting of the owls hooting society was held just outside the tent. To rub salt into the wound the only nocturnal flock of sheep in Wales decided to practice their yodelling skills all night long.

In the morning I told Dave, "That is the last time you or anyone else will get me within a mile of a tent."

***

On reaching the outskirts of Canterbury, the first notable building was the quaint St. Martin's church, part of a UNESCO World Heritage site. Apparently it is the first church founded in England and the oldest parish church still in use. How come I had never heard of it before? To build it, stones and tiles were recycled from earlier Roman buildings. This practice is called "Spoila". Not only was it regarded as good practice at the time but some spoila was seen to have mystical properties depending on where the material was taken from. Somehow I think it would be regarded as vandalism were we to use some of the stones from Stonehenge as spoila when constructing the next Sainsbury's store. Whilst wandering around the gravestones I noted one for John Neame. I would be visiting the Shepherd Neame brewery in Faversham shortly and wondered if this was a relative.

I needed to find a room for the night with ensuite facilities. Obviously, the Canterbury Club campsite was out of the question. So I headed for the tourist information centre cunningly disguised as the Beaney House of Art and Knowledge. It looked like an interesting place so made a mental note to visit it the next day.

Two millennia previously the three arms of Plautius's invasion force met up in Canterbury with the probable points of arrival into Britain being Lympne, Dover and Richborough. The army was numbered around 40,000, with it being made up of around 20,000 each of legionaries and auxiliaries. The base unit of a typical legion was the tent party. Eight men shared a tent which was carried by a mule that also transported the kettle and grindstone for milling the flour; bread and biscuits being the staple food for an army on the march. Ten tent parties, that is 80 men, made up a century commanded by a centurion. One thing that surprised me was that a centurion was in charge of 80 men and not 100.

Six centuries made up a cohort (480 men) and there were ten cohorts in a legion; the first cohort was double the size of the others. Add on 120 horsemen and officers and we get to around 5400 men. So there would have been the equivalent of just under four legions in Canterbury and an equal number of auxiliaries. Obviously, some men from the invasion force would have been allotted the task of maintaining the three bridgeheads on the coast. Nevertheless, we are talking about a heck of a lot of fertiliser produced by each legion and that is discounting the herd of elephants that Claudius would be bringing later.

That brings us nicely to the issue of sanitary arrangements. Have you noticed that in none of the sword and sandal epics nor the many westerns, we get any clue as to the toilet arrangements? The Roman army had to be well organised when it came to latrines. High ranks had private loos but most soldiers on the march used temporary public toilets. These hastily built facilities were sited near wells or streams. Larger, more permanent forts had proper aqueducts to support the toilets. For an army on the march the construction of the toilets would have been no more basic than wooden seats capable of being erected and dismantled quickly. You would want to be first in line as apparently the alternative to toilet paper was a sponge on a stick; both sponge and stick being shared. There were soldiers dedicated to the cleaning and maintenance of the facilities. Whilst we are on about toilet paper, how come Greece, a country that gave us an incredible civilisation and Alexander the Great, is still incapable of designing toilets that allow you to flush the paper down the loo?

Life would have been hard, I mean really hard, for the legionaries and auxiliaries, especially those allocated to latrine duties. Roman legionaries usually slept eight to a tent and definitely without the benefit of ensuite facilities and underarm deodorant. Yet there appeared to be no shortage of manpower. Officially, only unmarried Roman citizens could become legionaries. It should be noted that a Roman citizen need not have been born in Rome. People in conquered territories and client kingdoms sought the citizenship and rights associated with it.

Legionaries, carrying heavy equipment, could be expected to march around twenty miles a day on unmade roads. Each man would be responsible for their own fighting gear; a spear (pilum), sword and shield. They were a highly trained and disciplined fighting force. After 25 years they could retire as veterans. No less ferocious were the auxiliaries, non-Roman citizens, recruited from conquered tribes and allies. After 25 years they were granted Roman citizenship.

I spent the night in a hotel in the centre of Canterbury so did not have to spend it in the company of seven other legionaries in a tent. One cannot comprehend the aromas and noises percolating through the canvas. Then again if all eight legionaries smelt the same would they notice anything? I believe that Quentin Crisp once said that if you don't clean your house for four years it does not get any dirtier. In the bar at the hotel a gentleman from Singapore told me that some air hostesses clean their knickers in hotels by boiling them in the kettles in their rooms. As an ex-scientist I thought that I should test this idea so went back to my room and gave it a go. Be careful how much shampoo you put in the kettle as I covered the floor in froth. However, the experiment was a success and the added bonus is that for the next customer it did get rid of the lime scale that coats the kettles in the southeast of England. Whilst not sharing a tent with noisy legionaries I did have to listen to the antics coming from the room next door. My room had not been fitted with a trampoline, theirs' obviously had.

Before setting off on my tour of the city of Canterbury, I didn't seem to have time or enthusiasm to boil the kettle in my room to make the coffee for my flask. Anyway, there would be plenty of coffee houses in Canterbury to satisfy my caffeine dependency.

***

At the time of the Roman invasion of AD43, Canterbury was the administrative centre for the Cantiaci tribe, which was the dominant force in Kent. It would soon be the site of a Roman fort too. To most of us its historical fame comes from two factors; Geoffrey Chaucer's Canterbury Tales and the murder of the archbishop of Canterbury, Thomas Becket. However, long before Canterbury Cathedral became the centre of the Christian Church in Britain, the Romans had accepted Christianity in the Empire.

In the BBC's commentary on Christianity in Britain (BBC Religion website) it says that:

"In the 1st Century AD, Britain had its own set of religious icons: Pagan gods of the earth and Roman gods of the sky. Into this superstitious and violent world came a modern, fashionable cult from the east: Christianity ... a single religion with a single God appealed to the Roman Emperor Constantine. He saw that Christianity could be harnessed to unite his Empire and achieve military success. From 313 AD onwards, Christian worship was tolerated within the Roman Empire. During the 4th Century, British Christianity became more visible but it had not yet won over the hearts and minds of the population. Pagan beliefs still abounded and Christianity was a minority faith."

So, Christianity had a presence in Britain that was growing towards the end of the Roman occupation in the fifth century. With the invasion of Britain by the mainly Germanic tribes, however, there was a steady diminishing in the role of Christianity in the island. To help promote the authority of the Rome-based church, which conversely had become far stronger in mainland Europe, Pope Gregory sent St Augustine to the Island in AD597 and shortly after he converted the Kentish king Aethelbert to Christianity. In fact he was the first British king to be converted. For the next 1,000 years Roman Catholic Christianity became the dominant religion of Britain. Thomas Becket, the most famous of Canterbury cathedral's archbishops, was murdered there in 1170 by order of the then king, Henry II. Shortly after his death Thomas was canonised as a saint and Canterbury became a place of pilgrimage.

During the Reformation, in the reign of Henry VIII, Canterbury remained the centre of the Christian church in Britain after the break from the Roman Catholic Church. The Act of Supremacy in 1534 marked this final break with Rome. Even after this Thomas Becket was still revered and he has remained a hero for both

Catholic and Protestant branches of Christianity. Accordingly, Canterbury has maintained its status as a religious focal point.

Chaucer wrote his Canterbury Tales, from 1387 to 1400. It is written in Middle English as a collection of stories that each of the members of a pilgrimage from London to Canterbury relate to their travelling companions. The best tale would earn their narrator a free meal at the Tabard Inn in Southwark on their return. The fact that Chaucer uses pilgrims to tell the stories does not mean that there is any religious intent in the work. To be honest, some of the stories are bawdy and even teeter over the edge into the obscene. He could have quite easily called it Ilkley Tales, with people narrating stories whilst on a working men's club day out from Leeds to Ilkley.

Once I got my head around the fact that Canterbury Tales has little to do with Canterbury, what had been confusing me about the Pilgrims Way no longer confused me. Naively, I had assumed that it followed the route from London that is taken by Chaucer's pilgrims. Wrong. The Pilgrim's Way ends at Canterbury Cathedral but has nothing to do with the Roman route from London; it does not use Watling Street. It starts in Winchester, city and county town of Hampshire, far to the southwest of Canterbury and follows an ancient track that links these two cities. Here is further evidence that the Romans did not introduce the concept of roads to Britain.

So, aside from Chaucer and Becket what did Canterbury have to offer? Quite a lot as it happens, as befits one of the most visited towns in Britain by tourists. There is a UNESCO World Heritage site, which rather confusingly is based on three sites; the Cathedral, St Augustine's Abbey and St Martin's church (which I had visited the previous day). Whereas the cathedral and the church are working structures, St Augustine's is a ruin. Augustine is credited with founding the Catholic Church in England and became the first archbishop of Canterbury. The cathedral itself was completely rebuilt during the reign of William the Conqueror and added to and repaired over proceeding generations. There is no denying that this is a spectacular structure, the largest place of worship I had ever set foot in. It is well worth dodging the crowds for. No matter how busy these ancient places of worship are, I find that you can always find a quiet spot somewhere in them to slow things down.

If you want to avoid the mass of tourists I recommend a serene trip along the river Stour. As your small boat meanders past the university one can almost picture the more famous punting on the much wider Cam at Cambridge University. The Stour splits into two in Canterbury and then joins back into one again. Both gently flowing legs seemed to be no more than a foot deep. Another place away from tourists is the Roman museum. I popped in there for an hour and had the place to myself. Whether the entry price puts people off or that there are just so many other attractions competing for their custom, I can't say. Anyway, I was totally unprepared for how well the museum was laid out and the detail it provided. At the end of the circular route were the actual foundations of a Roman house and mosaic flooring. This place deserves to be as well visited as any of the other attractions that Canterbury has to offer.

Next stop was the free to enter Beaney House of Art and Knowledge, named after its main benefactor James Beaney, who donated £10,000 for the construction at the end of the nineteenth century. It is a combined tourist information centre, public library, and museum and art gallery. Having feasted myself on history and culture it was obvious that I should further improve my aesthetic credentials so went upstairs to see the Rupert Bear display. Rupert's connection with Canterbury is because his author, Mary Tourtel, lived and studied there. To my delight there was also a display of Bagpuss, the Clangers and Noggin the Nog. Oliver Postgate (with co-writer Peter Firmin) was one of my childhood heroes. He was responsible for these classics as well as Ivor the Engine and Pogles' Wood and did the voice overs for them. What I learned from my visit was that he was also an artist of some renown, painting the 50 feet long Illumination of the Life and Death of Thomas Becket.

There we go, back to Becket. I was lucky enough to see Postgate's drawing when an attendant kindly dug out a copy from the vault, or whatever you call a museum's hidden storeroom.

Canterbury is a city of incredible history and equally amazing buildings. It was a pleasure strolling through the cobbled streets looking at the 16th and 17th century timber framed buildings. Then something struck me. There were modern building in places that I would have expected the Tudor ones to be. Surely the planners had not been so crass as to demolish historic building and replace them with mid-20th century dross. No, we cannot blame the planners this time but Adolph Hitler. In March 1942 British bombers attacked the historic town of Lubeck in Germany. Most of the old town was destroyed. Hitler ordered retaliatory raids against historic places, raids which had little or no strategic value in terms of the war effort. These attacks became known as the Baedeker Blitz after Gustav Braun von Stumm declared on 24th April 1942 that:

> "We shall go out and bomb every building in Britain marked with three stars in the Baedeker guide".

Bath, Canterbury, Exeter, Norwich and York were the main targets. Canterbury cathedral suffered minor damage but surrounding buildings were destroyed. The Baedeker raids were soon stopped as the bombings with their associated loss of German planes and crew had little or no impact on morale.

***

Having completed my tour of what is an extremely beautiful city, despite its often crowded streets, I was ready for the next stage. The official start of Watling Street is regarded as Dover and at Canterbury I was now on Watling Street proper and would remain so until I reached London. Incidentally, it is believed that Watling Street gets its name from the Old English Waecelinga Street (with the Waecelingas being a tribe from the St Albans area). We tend to think of streets as urban roads but strata in Latin meant any road, urban or rural.

I loaded up my rucksack, set off and after about half a mile realised that the heavy rucksack was no longer a problem. My body had already got used to the weight. With this realisation I had an extra spring in my step. Actually, I think that I have found a cure for bad backs too as mine felt fine. Treatment: walk around for a few hours each day with a 15 kilo pack on your back.

3 CANTERBURY TO ROCHESTER

Route: Margary 1b (pages 42-44).

On a recent walking holiday in Alsace in France, I used the Eurostar high speed rail link through the Channel Tunnel for the first time. Half an hour through customs and security, two and a half hours from London to Paris and the same again from Paris to Colmar and I was in the heart of Alsace. As I passed through the French countryside at almost 200 miles per hour, I could not help musing about what an amazing thing the high speed rail link is and how it compared to a Roman's passage through Gaul. I think that the gentle swaying of the train may have caused me to nod off as I was suddenly transported back to Kent.

Canterbury planning office AD43. Aulus Plautius enters the office. Sitting there are the planning officer and his clerk Borthrum.

Clerk   'Ere, look what the cat's dragged in. That bloke's wearing a dress sir.

Planning Officer Thank you Borthrum. I think that is what the continentals call a toga.

Clerk   They can call it what they like, it is still a dress to me. No self-respecting Celt would be seen dead in one of them.

Planning Officer Keep your voice down, he may hear you.

Clerk   Ee up. 'Ere comes the geezer.

Plautius approaches the desk

Planning Officer Can I help you sir?

Plautius   I am looking to construct a high speed cart track from Dubris to Londinium.

Clerk   Never heard of them mate.

Plautius   Ah, I think that you will call them Dover and London.

Planning Officer I know Dover sir, but where is London?

Plautius   *(stating proudly)* It will be the site of the Roman Empire's provincial capital in Britannia.

Ignoring this grand statement, the planning officer pulls a form from a drawer.

Planning Officer Okay sir, can I take a few details, please? Name and occupation?

Plautius   Aulus Plautius, Roman general.

Clerk   I thought that wasn't a local accent. Er, have you come far?

Plautius   Originally from Rome, the greatest city in the known world.

Planning Officer Oh. I've never been abroad sir. I don't think the hot weather would suit me. I prefer the cool rain of a British summer and the cold snow of our winters.

Clerk   I've heard the food is rubbish too, all fish sauce, olives and warm white wine. Now, you can't beat a gourmet dish of jellied eels or pie, mash and liquor washed down with a pint of foaming beer.

Plautius   And what is liquor?

Clerk   A mucus coloured gravy made from eels. Delicious.

Planning Officer And where did you arrive in Britannia, sir?

Plautius   Richborough, on the coast, about twenty miles from here. Came over via Gaul a few days ago.

Planning Officer May I see your entry visa, sir?

Plautius   I don't have one.

Planning Officer Hmm. Need to get a visa filled out general. Anyway let's carry on. Purpose of visit, sir?

Plautius   Invasion and subjugation of Britannia.

Clerk   Yeh, sure, you and whose army mate?

Plautius   Well, mine actually.

The planning officer looks surprised.

Planning Officer And how many are there in this army, sir?

Plautius   About 20,000 legionaries and 20,000 auxiliaries.

Clerk   Bloody Boudicca!

Plautius   What? Who?

Clerk   Boudicca, Queen of the Iceni tribe. Her mates call her Boadicea. Nasty piece of work if she gets upset. A superstitious lady too. Her soothsayer has looked at the runes and predicted that within twenty years she will decimate an invading army that has something to do with the number nine.

Plautius   Well I have the Ninth Legion but they are the pride of the Empire so it can't be anything to do with them.

Planning Officer That's as maybe sir. Can we get back to the matter in hand?

The *clerk turns to the planning officer.*

Clerk   That is going to dent our immigration figures boss. Have to hide those details somehow. You know how keen our chief is to keep net immigration down. This country is already getting overcrowded if you ask me.

Planning Officer Okay, thank you Borthrum.

But the clerk ignores him and carries on.

Clerk   Soon us Celts will be outnumbered. All we need is for the Angles and Saxons to try to sneak in and the next thing you know the country will change its name to Angland or something like that. God forbid that they ever build a bridge or tunnel to get from Gaul to here.

Planning Officer Yes, thank you Borthrum.

Clerk   And what will happen to us, I ask you? Probably be forced from our homes and end up in some God forsaken place far to the west eating leeks and daffodils. Or, even worse, we could be driven north and end up eating thistles and haggis. Haggis is offal if you ask me.

Plautius   Look, I came to tell you that I am going to construct a high speed cart track from Dubris to Londinium.

Clerk   Yeh, well that's as may be mate. Any other immigrants planned?

Plautius   Well Emperor Claudius will be coming in a couple of months to lead the advance on Camulodunum, Colchester to you.

Planning Officer And will he be bringing much with him, sir?

Plautius   Not too many men, but he will be bringing a herd of elephants with him.

Planning Officer What are elephants, sir?

Plautius   Big animals, with four legs, tusks and a trunk. Size of a hut. They put the fear of the gods into our enemies. Will make your chariots look weedy.

Clerk   Well, we can't have them entering the country without spending six months in quarantine. We have very strict quarantine laws on this side of the Channel. Can't have the country flooded with rabid animals can we? Also, you will have to follow behind these creatures with buckets ... bloody big buckets. We should have a slogan for that. "Scoop the Poop" or something like that.

Planning Officer Thank you Borthrum, I will dig out the quarantine paperwork later. Right, general, let us get back to the immediate matter in hand, sir. With regards to the building of a high speed cart track.

Plautius   We call them Roman roads in Italy.

Planning Officer That's as maybe, sir. Have you had the obligatory three months consultation period allowing you time to discuss the implications of this track with representatives from all the communities that the track will pass through?

Plautius   Well, no.

Clerk   Hah! Thought not. And have you come up with a compensation package for those whose huts will be demolished or blighted by this blot on the landscape?

Plautius can contain himself no longer and storms out of the room shouting ...

Plautius   By Jupiter and Neptune, sod this for a game of legionaries. I'm not taking any more of this nonsense. I've got an island to conquer and your petty bureaucracy is not going to stand in my way.

The clerk turns to the planning officer.

Clerk   Bunch of barbarians, these Romans, if you ask me boss.

***

As Plautius and his army departed from Canterbury heading for a suitable crossing over the Thames, he and his men must have thought that things were quiet … too quiet! The landing at the three points of entry into Britain and the march to Canterbury had been relatively straightforward. How long would this last? Where were the enemy? Who were the enemy?

Let us consider what Britain in the southeast was like prior to the Roman invasion. Barry Cunliffe, gives an excellent countdown to the invasion and also looks at what happened when the Romans departed, never to return after 400 years of imperial rule. He sets the scene well in "Britain Begins" (pages 35-75). Traces of pre homo-sapiens species in Britain date back 500,000 years but there is evidence of their stone-age activities (flint implements and butchered animal carcasses) that pushes this back to 900,000 years ago. Ice ages came and went with ice sheets covering most of Britain, wiping out any indigenous populations of hominids. Evidence of homo-sapiens in Africa dates this new species to around 150,000 years ago with traces excavated in Britain showing evidence of their presence here to around 40,000 years ago. Then the Last Glacial Maximum covered most of Britain in an ice sheet about a mile thick. So much water was locked in as ice that the southern North Sea and English Channel became dry lowlands. Humans could not survive in Britain. Around 15,000 years ago the steady warming of the climate of northern Europe allowed for migration back north into southern Britain. So we have 15,000 years of human development in the area that the Romans were seeking to conquer.

At the time of the Roman invasion, Britain was a series of independent tribes, each intent on maintaining their slice of the cake and occasionally taking someone else's. The contents of the slices were dependent on where in Britain the tribes were situated. Some areas were rich in minerals and the highly prized gold and silver, others had excellent farming land and some tribes had the best of both worlds. Through trading links, in Britain and with their Roman neighbours on the continent, most tribes were able to provide for their peoples' needs. Alliances were preferable to fighting over the slices. However, as is ever the case when it comes to the human race, infighting amongst the Britons took place to ensure more favourable conditions. Communication links were slow as the limited number of poorly maintained tracks that covered Britain at the time did not favour the rapid movement of people and information and superfast broadband was not quite ready to be rolled out. Come to think of it, superfast broadband has still not reached many rural communities.

Whilst historians disagree over the exact position in AD43 I will plumb for the following simplified version. South of the Thames were the Cantiaci (in Kent) and the Atrebates (in Sussex). North of the Thames were the Catuvellauni. The Dubunni were west of the Thames. The Atrebates formed an alliance with the Romans and the Dubunni surrendered before any major battle took place. The Cantiaci allied with the Catuvellauni under the leadership of brothers, Togodumnus and Caratacus (see the battle of Medway later in this chapter). It would have taken time to mobilise sufficient force for the Britons to feel that they could confront the Roman army. Thus after landing the Romans only had to contend with minor skirmishes and guerrilla tactics. So they started their march from Canterbury to London relatively unmolested. And I set off from Canterbury along Watling Street relatively unmolested too. But that was to change in less than three miles.

***

Watling Street, mainly the modern A2 road from Canterbury to Rochester is for the most part an almost straight line. In fact Margary (page 42) describes it thus;

> *"Except for a few trifling variations of line, this road runs on a practically direct alignment between the two terminals. This is partly due to the easy nature of the country through which it goes, but it was, of course, the most important thoroughfare in Roman Britain, and nearly all those who came to the island Province must have travelled along it to the capital."*

I started my walk at Canterbury castle, an old Norman ruin and then headed for Harbledown on the outskirts of town as this was the probable route of the old Roman road out of the city. Once through Harbledown I went along a road conveniently called Roman Road and, having got Margary's trifling variations out of the way, eventually got to the straight bit.

I was about to get molested. Every so often we do things that are totally out of character and defy any logic. Passing a place called Paintballing.co.uk, on a whim I popped in to see what it was all about. To the uninitiated this involves dressing up in combat gear and then spending the time wandering about splattering (and being splattered by) people you don't know with blobs of paint. It is crass, meaningless and caters to the baser instincts of juveniles and men suffering from a mid-life crisis. I was persuaded to have a go and endured it for what seemed an age. Males of the species were running around, testosterone levels at maximum, blasting anyone they came in contact with. It was great fun. If this was a mid-life crisis then I would live until I was 130 years of age.

Having got paintballing out of my system I needed tranquillity so I strolled on to Dunkirk where I assumed there would be a church on a hill. And there was, well almost. There is a small hill but no church. To be more precise the church was now a house. This required further delving. The church was built in 1840 but then declared redundant in 1988. A surplus to requirements church suggested to me one of two things; falling attendance or the people in the area were now so saintly that they no longer needed a regular holy fix. Sadly, it is not the latter.

All the buildings in Dunkirk are Victorian or later. But why was a church built in such a quiet place? Answer, because it wasn't always a quiet leafy location. Now I am not making any of the following up. In 1838, Dunkirk was the scene of the last armed rising on English soil. Local character Sir William Courtenay was concerned with the conditions of farm workers who were becoming destitute with the introduction of mechanisation. Unable to gain a seat in parliament to fight the cause he stirred up the locals. The army was called out and easily defeated Courtenay's force in Bossenden Wood. The battle resulted in the death of Courtenay, seven of his men and two soldiers. Two of his following were transported to Australia where one made a fortune in the gold fields (clouds and silver linings springs to mind). The episode became national news. The government took "decisive" action by setting up a Christian mission and built a church and school in Dunkirk.

There is a poignant footnote to this story. A former pupil of the school, Jack Cornwell, fought at the battle of Jutland and for his bravery was awarded the Victoria Cross posthumously.

Keeping to the line of the Roman road (and not the A2 which bypasses Dunkirk) I walked into Boughton. As I was passing St Barnabas Parish Centre, I saw a road sign to Selling and decided that a one mile detour could be fitted into my itinerary. I could not resist visiting Selling, England for the reason that my favourite album is Selling England by the Pound by Genesis. And I was mighty glad that I paid it a visit. The village and the road to it are a plethora of grade I and II listed buildings, including St Mary's church which was compact yet rather beautiful. Oast houses and orchards made me feel that this is why Kent is called the Garden of England. I had a mid-morning snack at the grade II listed White Lion pub and then retraced my steps back to Boughton, listening to Genesis on my iPod.

The road from Canterbury to Boughton had been lined with what were obviously orchards of fruit trees. On the way to Faversham I now passed fields with large upright poles with wires strung across them. I had no idea what they were for. I would soon find out.

My next stopping point on the Roman road was the sizeable town of Faversham. It was previously the centre of the explosives industry until an accident killed over 100 workers in 1916, knocking off the roofs of many houses in the town in the process. Also, with its link to the Swale and the Thames Estuary, there is evidence throughout the town of Faversham's maritime past. Abbey Street is particularly steeped in history and there are numerous plaques on houses along the street providing interesting detail. King Stephen was buried in the Abbey and then his remains dug up and allegedly moved to an unmarked grave in the local church. This seems a rather low key end to the last Norman king of England. The only part that remains of the Abbey is Arden House. In 1551 its owner, Thomas Arden, was more interested in making money than keeping his wife amused so she got her lover to kill him in the house. Both she and her lover were executed for the crime. At number 89 Abbey Street there lived a man who had a very varied existence. Michael Greenwood was press ganged in 1748. Ten years later he was shipwrecked off Morocco and sold into slavery, ransomed after two years and then returned to Faversham where he no doubt spent the rest of his eighty years wining and dining on his exploits.

Being on Watling Street, Faversham (Durolevum) has a Roman history too. Various artefacts dating to the Roman occupation have been found including coins, urns and the remains of buildings. By far the most spectacular find was in 2013 when, on a hill close to the town, a 2,000 year old auditorium was unearthed. This outdoor theatre is thought to be the earliest Roman one to be discovered in England. Unlike amphitheatres like the Coliseum, with their stages in the centre, the Faversham one had its stage at one end in traditional theatre style. It could hold 12,000 people in 50 rows and may have been used for religious festivals as well as entertainment. Bronze Age artefacts have been discovered in this area also.

Faversham is better known (to me anyway) as the home of the Kent Police museum. My Dad was a police officer in England for thirty years so I had an inkling to visit the museum. The museum was opened in Chatham dockyard in an old boiler house in 1994. It closed in 2014 and eventually moved to Faversham police station. I popped into the station and asked the police to help me with my enquiries. Sadly, it is still in the development stage and is not planned to be opened until 2018. So there was nothing else for it but pop across the road to the Shepherd Neame Brewery.

When a science teacher at the local secondary school, I lived near Cockermouth in Cumbria and went on the Jennings brewery tour on a number of occasions. This was purely for scientific purposes, you understand, as the brewery was keen to explain the science of brewing before they forced the visitors to partake in the beer tasting. I now had an opportunity to expand my knowledge at Shepherd Neame (we should always seek to broaden our horizons as well as our waistlines). This is the oldest brewery in England and Faversham's major employer. The tours start at 14.00 pm and luckily I was able to get onto that day's tour. There was a notice that said that anyone wearing high heeled shoes would not be allowed on the tour. Luckily I was wearing my walking boots so was allowed in. I got to taste the water from the brewery's own well. Not being a connoisseur of these things I thought that it tasted just like water. The tour took us through to the Old Brewery Store, a wonderful trip down memory lane with regards to the brewing industry in the area. I found out that those fields of poles with wires were the hop fields. In the summer the hops would grow up ten to twelve feet using the poles and wires as support. I also learnt the difference between ale and beer. Ale contains only three ingredients (malt, water and yeast) whereas beer contains a fourth, hops. Hops were a continental addition to the British brewing process some time ago and have remained an integral ingredient. So the Campaign for Real Ale should be called the Campaign for Real Beer. With the educational side over then came the obligatory tasting of beers and lagers. The tour guide, John, explained how to get the most out of the tasting of the six different brews. We then had the opportunity to test in bulk. As I needed to crack on with my journey and find a B and B closer to Sittingbourne I had to be careful how much I tested. However, the tour was both enjoyable and informative and stimulated my thirst for knowledge and that thirst needed quenching. So I bulk tested some of the Shepherd Neame beers in the excellent Sun Inn. My favourite was the Whitstable stout.

During my session in the Sun I read that during the explosion in the gunpowder factory, the bedrooms on the second floor had been destroyed; blown away to be more precise. The next morning I awoke in a very plush second floor bedroom. Rather than pushing on towards Sittingbourne, I hadn't even made it out of the hotel. Feeling rather fuzzy headed, I could only face a light continental breakfast before departing the Sun Inn. Outside it was anything but sunny. A westerly wind was blowing stinging rain into my face. The weather matched my countenance. To keep away from the spray of the traffic on the A2 I used Lower Road to get to Teynham. I had recently had my first annual flu jab and a pneumonia injection, all courtesy of the National Health Service. In my pre-walk research, nowhere had it suggested that I should have anti-malaria treatment too. Whilst sheltering from the rain and drinking a very welcome hot cuppa, in the tea shop (Mrs T's Cakes) I chatted to a local and was gleefully informed that until recently malaria had been a common occurrence due to the presence of badly drained marshes nearby. How recently, I wondered? Apparently, draining of the marshes in the 1950's had put a stop to risk of the disease. I was unaware that malaria had ever been an issue in England. On leaving the tea shop I wandered around the village, keeping a keen eye out for mosquitos. Then again it was raining so heavily by this time that no self-respecting mosquito would be seen dead in it. At this rate the marshes would soon need to be drained again.

Cursing the incessant downpour I trudged on westwards, still using Lower Road until I reached Tonge. My heart was not in it, so quickly passing the old mill pond on my right I crossed the A2 and arrived at Bapchild. The old English for Bapchild is Beccanceld which means moist and bleak, a perfect description of me at that time. (Moist and damp mean the same thing, so how come we like moist fruit cake but not damp fruit cake?) More to keep out of the rain than anything else, I went into the grade I listed church of St Laurence. I managed to stretch my visit to half an hour during which time I noticed some 16th century graffiti near the south door. On leaving the church, my spirits somewhat lifted, I re-joined the A2 and strode purposefully into and equally as purposefully, straight out of Sittingbourne. In the past this town seems to have been used merely as a through point and I was doing the same. It was ignored in Domesday Book but then became a stopping point for pilgrims following the death of Thomas Becket. Henry V stayed there on his way back from Agincourt. Please note, I appreciate that modern Sittingbourne does have a life apart from being a thoroughfare but when you are cold and wet there is little enthusiasm to linger.

And so I pushed on past Newington and then to Rainham, another town name that seemed to match the day perfectly. This was as good a place as any to stop for the night. At least it would give me the chance to take off my wet clothes and try to dry out. My walking boots were rather soggy inside. I had now entered the urban sprawl that is made up of Rainham, Gillingham, Chatham and Rochester. This was the first time since leaving Richborough that I no longer felt in the Garden of England. This was still Kent but more like the Back Yard of England. I was hemmed in by the M2 to the south and the Medway to the north and west. Rainham was a sleepy settlement until the coming of the railway in the mid-19th century. The railway acted like spokes emanating from London. Along those spokes industry and housing grew to satisfy the never ending needs of the capital. The next morning, wearing my training shoes instead of my walking boots which were too damp to put on, I made rapid progress through the incessant urban sprawl from Rainham to Rochester via Chatham, bypassing Gillingham (which the Roman road does anyway). I would spend time in Chatham and Rochester the following day. The incessant rain of the previous day had stopped too and I was treated to wall to wall sunshine for the next eight hours.

* * *

In Rochester I was close to the historic battle of Medway, the first pitched battle that Aulus Plautius and his army fought on British soil. This is arguably one of the pivotal battles on this island as it led to 400 years of Roman rule. Had Britannia been allowed to evolve in isolation how different would the land look and feel today?

And that takes us nicely to the Britons that the Romans now faced. Let us start with the name Britain. In the Celtic language the letters P and B seemed to be interchangeable. Pretani probably comes from the Celtic term "painted ones". So the Bretani may have got their name from the woad they seemed to enjoy slapping all over their bodies. The Anglo Saxon Chronicle talks about Bretwalda, which is translated as ruler of Britain. We have a similar linguistic link with Bretons from Brittany where many Celts came from.

By the time the Romans reached the Medway their foe had been able to muster a force that they believed could drive the Roman army back to Gaul. Some sources suggest that the Romans were outnumbered three to one. The Celts were commanded by brothers Togodumnus and Caratacus. As Julius Caesar had noted almost a hundred years previously, chariots were an important element of the Celtic army. They still were. Not only could they intimidate the enemy but they were a rapid way of moving troops from one part of a battlefield to another and to bring in reinforcements.

The exact location of the battle is not known precisely but is assumed to lie somewhere along the Medway between modern day Aylesford and Chatham. The Roman legions would have lined up along the east bank of the river on a non-tidal stretch. It has been suggested that Batavian auxiliaries (strong swimmers who were trained to swim in full battle dress) crossed further upstream and surprised the enemy and wounded the horses that pulled the chariots. This forced the Celts to fight on foot.

Next, elite troops reached the west bank of the Medway at an easily fordable place that offered some natural protection from counter attack. The area near Snodland has been suggested. Two days of attack and counter attack ensued with the Romans finally claiming the victory. The remnants of Caratacus's beaten army retreated back across the Thames marshes towards their tribal capital of Camulodunum (Colchester). Togodumnus did not survive the battle. The Romans were unsure of these tidal waters so were unable to chase after the Celts. There have been many key battles over the centuries, on land, sea and air, which have helped shape the Britishness of this island. Medway should be ranked among them.

***

So, having got the battle out of the way, Aulus and his men readied themselves for the march to the Catuvellauni capital, Camulodunum. Having put much of the Celtic army to rout at the Medway, destruction of the administrative capital would lead to a dramatic effect on the morale of not only the Catuvellauni but also other British tribes. In many conflicts since the Roman invasion, taking over a capital has generally been seen as a crucial step in conquest and subjugation.

Before my march on London and Colchester I had places to see in Chatham and Rochester, but first I booked a room in the Horseshoe and Castle in Cooling. Yes, I know that I was really going off the straight and narrow to get to my accommodation; Cooling is three miles due north of Rochester, as the crow flies. However, getting from Rochester to Marble Arch along Watling Street would be, according to Margary, a trek of 33.5 miles, most of which would be through more urban and suburban blight and occasionally close to the busy A2. I was craving my last taste of rural Kent without being hampered by the incessant rain of the previous day. According to my Ordnance Survey map my journey to Cooling would be through verdant farmland and orchards, probably looking even more vibrant following the recent unceasing downpour. Sadly, I soon had an immense drop in morale.

If only I could have been like that proverbial crow. What started out as a three mile leisurely stroll ended up as a nightmare seven miles slog, during which I feared for my life. Popping over the

Medway Bridge at Rochester I aimed for the village of Chattenden. From there the route to Cooling was an almost straight line consisting of one clearly marked road and an equally clearly marked footpath. With confidence I marched through Chattenden. As indicated on my map, the road changed to a lane which then changed to a path. Unfortunately, what my map forgot to inform me was that there was a huge wall and metal gate stopping me from getting onto the path. There was an equally large sign which said "Ministry of Defence, No Entry".

I had no option but to retrace my steps and seek a route around the MOD site. The map indicated a number of paths but each one had an MOD sign prohibiting my access. Ending up back in Rochester I decided to aim for Cliffe along the B2000 and then cut across to Cooling. To my mind a walk along a B road through Kentish farmland would be some compensation for the abortive attempt to get to my overnight stop. The B2000 meanders gently up and down with blind bends every hundred yards or so. Unfortunately what else meandered down this lane were numerous juggernauts, all believing that the 40mph sign was a minimum and not a limit. Surely they could not all be heading for Cliffe? If so, Cliffe must be a highly industrialised town. There was no footpath either. Keeping as close to the hedgerow as possible, and occasionally being blown into it, I gingerly made my way, fearing for my life. I reached the Mockbeggar farm shop and tea room and went inside with the intention of having a much needed cuppa and then getting a taxi for the last four miles to Cooling.

A couple were the only other customers in the tea room. As I entered, shaking and sweating profusely from the concentration needed to survive the walk of death, the man asked me cheerfully, "Having a nice walk?" In as casual a manner as I could muster, I explained that, despite the lovely sunny weather I could not walk another step along that highway from Hell and that I was hoping for someone to phone for a taxi. I sat down and had a strong cup of tea and a huge slice of delicious lemon drizzle cake. Is it just the British who appreciate the healing properties of a cuppa? Unknown to me, an angel named Georgette, disguised as the owner of the tea room, had heard my conversation and said that if I was willing to wait half an hour then she would drive me to my hotel. This was the sort of person I could wait my whole life for. Disregarding the maxim "Don't take lifts from strangers", I readily accepted and only just avoided offering to marry this ministering angel. Avoiding the other maxim "Don't offer lifts to strangers", Georgette happily drove out of her way and dropped me off at the pub. She had possibly saved my life.

And what a wonderful pub it was. The Horseshoe and Castle is the only hostelry in the tiny village of Cooling. It was quite busy too. Beer and food were excellent and the service superb. Whilst eating my meal in the bar, I found out that the pub is a meeting place for farmers who like to come in after a hard day's graft. One of the farmers owns a pumpkin farm and near to Halloween he gets up to three thousand visitors a day picking their pumpkins. Why did pumpkins suddenly ring a bell? Of course, I had seen the elephants at Howletts eating some. I would hate to be a visitor to the farm on the day the elephants came to pick their own. Other people in the bar were from the RSPB, each explaining to the others how their day had gone. I had a splendid time people watching and completely forgot about the horrendous journey of the day. After a long hot shower I sunk into my bed. Tomorrow I would get back onto the straight and narrow but couldn't face walking down the dreaded B2000 again to get there.

4 ROCHESTER TO LONDON (MARBLE ARCH)

Route: Margary 1c (pages 51-52).

In the morning I awoke to the sound of a myriad small birds, all chattering together, each one intent on talking and not listening. They reminded me of the conversations in the bar the night before. All of a sudden there was a gunshot in the distance and the birds went silent. Five seconds later in perfect unison, the cacophony started up again, each bird obviously continuing with their tale as if there had been no interruption. I found this highly amusing.

After breakfast, having perused my mainly reliable Ordnance Survey map, I decided to walk across the fields from Cooling to Cliffe using part of the long distance footpath, the Saxon Shore Way, and then get a bus to the Medway, so avoiding the B2000. Firstly though, I explored Cooling. St James church is no longer a working church but well worth a visit. In the graveyard is a series of tiny coffin shaped gravestones.

These were Dicken's inspiration when he described the death of Pip's siblings in Great Expectations. Also, Magwitch is supposed to have jumped out at Pip from behind a large gravestone at the rear of the churchyard. The actual graves mark the resting place of thirteen children from two families. They are believed to have died from malaria. So, with regards to the local person I met in the previous chapter in Teynham's tea shop, where she gleefully told me of the risk of malaria, she wasn't having me on.

Belying the statement that any publicity is good publicity, Edward Hastead in "The History of Kent" in 1797 said,

> "Cowling [another name for Cooling] *is an unfrequented place, the roads of which are deep and miry and it is as unhealthy as it is unpleasant".*

Unsurprising it was unfrequented with publicity like that. It is frequented now by Jools Holland, a musician hero of mine. He really has taken "my home is my castle" literally as he lives in Cooling castle.

Whilst on the subject of castles, I have never been in a bouncy castle. They do look fun but are really designed for children. To celebrate my nephew Tom's twelfth birthday one was erected in his back garden. He and his pals were having a great time until my sister Joy, then in her mid-forties, decided to join them. Rather than crawl into the castle she threw herself onto it. As she bounced on so Tom and his friends bounced off, having first been launched about three feet into the air. From a spectator's point of view it looked highly amusing. My nephew probably thought otherwise, as he has not ventured into a bouncy castle since.

Close to the pub I took a small track north and within less than a mile was into the heart of the marshes. What a wonderful place, bleak but beautiful. It is a bird sanctuary and nature reserve and long may it remain so. Two miles away, the Thames estuary was visible and the whole of the area before me was mine and mine alone. The silence was gently counterpointed by distant calls of the marsh birds and the far off drone of a tractor. Though this wasn't his neck of the woods, I recalled my favourite classical composer, Vaughan Williams. His third symphony (pastoral) would not be out of place here. Also, I could imagine Dickens seeing a similar area like this near to Gravesend and rushing home to write the opening of Great Expectations, describing Pip's first meeting with Magwich who had escaped from a prison hulk moored in the estuary. David Lean's film of the book starts with an evocative scene of the lonely windswept marshland and I was now living it, albeit in colour.

Snapping out of my rural reverie, I continued my stroll from Cooling to Cliffe and passed through vast strawberry fields and huge pear orchards. The pears weren't huge you understand, just the orchards. The strawberry fields seemed to go on forever. It would have been perfect if I had been walking along Penny Lane as this was the Beatle's double A-sided single that included Strawberry Fields Forever on the other side. Sadly, no lanes with this name. Every so often I came across lines of tall hedges. The previously far off tractor was close by now and a farm worker with an eastern European accent dismounted and ambled over. He explained that these trees were windbreaks which were essential in such a flat and exposed area. It was he who pointed out the pear trees, explaining that they were top quality conference pears grown for the supermarkets. I am not a lover of pears. When you buy them they are rock hard. By the time they are soft enough to eat you have gone off the idea of eating them. It is better to keep stocks of bottled fruit as these can be opened anytime. My favourites are merlot and sauvignon blanc.

On arriving at Cliffe it was obviously a sleepy village. The large parish church of St Helen's was named after the daughter of the first Christian Roman emperor, Constantine. The demonic B2000 ends abruptly here yet there was no sign of any lorries ever having arrived. Had I imagined my walk with death the previous day? Was I suffering from heatstroke? During my research a couple of references in the Higham Parish Council annual newsletter of 2017 convinced me that I had not imagined things. In the section written by the Dickens Country Protection Society, they say

> *"Housing developments proposed in Cliffe Woods: The society is aware of planning applications to erect 50 dwellings on farmland to the south and a further 225 to the west of Cliffe Woods. The Society has objected to the latter application. There are concerns about increased traffic on the B2000 ..."*

Also, in the Higham Neighbourhood Forum (HNF) section it is pointed out that

> *"The Forum also runs Speed Watch which is one of several schemes which monitors traffic speeds throughout Kent. Although no drivers are prosecuted persistent offenders do receive a letter from the Police reminding them of the dangers of speeding."*

I recommend that the B2000 requires the constant attention of HNF. I also recommend the reading of the parish newsletter for its insight into the goings on in a small rural English village. Further research undertaken showed me that close to Cliffe is "the largest independent producer of sand and gravel in the UK with quarry, marine dredged aggregates and coated roadstone operations serving London, the East and South East of England" (as quoted in their website). Ah, does this explain the number of juggernauts on the B2000?

The bus journey from Cliffe to the Medway took about ten minutes. Alighting just to the west of the river, I made my way to Upnor castle. From the Elizabethan fort's battlements I looked across the river towards Chatham dockyard which I would be visiting shortly. The fort was built to protect warships that were moored in the docks. In typical English self-effacing style, the Upnor castle website says,

> "Despite a brave attempt, it entirely failed to do so in 1667, when the Dutch sailed past it to burn or capture the English fleet at anchor."

We are told about the proud naval traditions of our fleet, including the victory at Trafalgar and the draw at Jutland. No-one mentions Chatham. In this battle the Dutch started by attacking and taking Sheerness further up the coast (who thought that the battle of Hastings was the last invasion of these shores?). Then their fleet advanced along the Medway, cutting the metal chain that was strung across the river and which was supposed to prevent ships getting any further. They were able to destroy a number of ships at anchor and then rubbed salt into the wounds by boarding the English flagship and taking it back to their home port. I find it hard to comprehend that the castle was unable to blow the Dutch ships out of the water. Some of the cannons I saw were pretty big to say the least (see below), and the castle had an uninterrupted view across the Medway. We are talking sitting ducks here, less than a quarter of a mile away. Furthermore the gun crews did not have to contend with the rise and fall of the waves. King Charles II was less than impressed when he found out that the flagship, HMS Royal Charles, was converted into a tourist attraction by the Dutch. Charles must have felt a proper Charley. A contemporary account of the devastating raid was written by non other than Samuel Pepys, he of the diary fame. At the time he was the secretary of the Navy Board. An entry in his diary states:

"I do fear so much that the whole kingdom is undone, that I do this night resolve to study with my father and wife what to do with the little that I have in money by me"

Which roughly translates as "This country is buggered. Hide the family silver". Having failed as a means of protection, the castle was converted to a gunpowder store and remained so for many years to come.

On leaving the castle I walked up a narrow cobbled street. I could imagine strains of "Yo, ho, ho and a bottle of rum" floating through the air whilst locals were running for their lives from the press gangs. Seeking safety, I popped into the Tudor Rose and had a pint of Proper Job and a bag of ye olde cheese and onion crisps.

Next on my agenda was the Historic Dockyard of Chatham. Now this is a big museum, and I do mean huge, as befits somewhere that celebrates Britain's maritime history. It is on a different scale to the no less impressive Imperial War museum that I would be visiting later in this chapter. It is extremely kids friendly but also very informative for those seeking education as well as the opportunity to prod, poke and run wild. I allowed myself three hours (including lunch) and could in all honesty have spent longer there. There is much variety, including Victorian (see below) and WW2 ships and a late 20th century submarine to stroll around and through. The submarine was the last ship to be built at Chatham in 1962. For the super nerds there is a Victorian ropery that tells you all you need to know about making rope. Chatham struck me as a town seeking an identity. Its glory days coincided with the inception, expansion and maintenance of the British Empire. As the Empire dwindled to nothing more than a historical irrelevance so Chatham lost its main reason for being. As with Britain in general and many old fishing and maritime communities in particular, it is living on past memories.

I retraced my steps back through Chatham and using High Street made my way to Rochester. After the urban and industrial sprawl that I had encountered since reaching Rainham I was expecting to see little of interest. How wrong could I be? First stop, King's School which was founded in AD604. This school is the second oldest continuously running school in the world (the Kings School in Canterbury having opened seven years previously). I rather like their no nonsense motto, "Learn or Leave". I looked and left. Literally a stone's throw from the school is Rochester cathedral, which was also started in the same year. School and cathedral have been linked ever since. Whereas the original building has long since disappeared, the striking Norman building stands proud in all its grandeur. A priest called Gundulf was appointed its first Norman bishop. I wonder if Tolkien based his wizard Gandalf on this priest. There was a team of keen volunteers on hand and I recommend the free of charge (donations gladly accepted) twenty minutes highlights tour. As mentioned in chapter 2, Canterbury cathedral became a place of pilgrimage following the death of Thomas Becket. He had been the second most powerful man in the kingdom after Henry II. Prior to becoming archbishop of Canterbury, Beckett was Lord Chancellor. Plays and films have been made about him. He had an impressive CV. It is less well known that Rochester cathedral also became a place of pilgrimage during the 13th century following the death nearby of William of Perth, a baker. They must love their bread in Rochester.

Winding my way through the cobbled streets I reached Rochester castle, which remained a strategic and working fortress for over 500 years since it was built by the Normans. I wandered around the site, and having climbed to the top of the battlements, took in the wonderful views across the Medway and of the cathedral. From here I could also see the modern dual carriageway across the river and couldn't help but compare this view with the photograph in Helen Livingston's book "Kent – Pictorial Memories". This evocative book is full of photographs of towns and villages in Kent dating from Victorian times to the mid twentieth century. They include places I had already visited on my walk; Littlebourne's mill on the Stour pictured in 1903, Faversham's West Street in 1892 and the view across the Medway in Rochester in 1889. Helen wrote an informative book on Roman roads too (see references). The bridge in Helen's book forms one half of the modern dual carriageway but it has been substantially strengthened. With Rochester having the suffix -chester I expected to find some ruins of the Roman fortress that would have been built. The closest I got was when I found out that the castle was built using stones from the original Roman city walls.

Eastgate House museum marks the easterly boundary of the old Roman town. The museum is well worth a visit. Following a £2.2 million Heritage Lottery Fund grant, this impressive 16th/17th century building was reopened only recently to the public in July 2017 and I got full value for money for my £4 entry fee (concession rate). The building has been at various times a family residence, a young men's hostel (cue YMCA by the Village People), a temperance restaurant, a Charles Dickens centre and a private boarding school. One of the upper rooms is decked out as a school room equipped with a knowledgeable lady wielding a cane. One of the well to do scallywags had scratched some graffiti on a pane of glass "Sarah Couchman came here 21st Jany (January) 1797". Perhaps this was the inspiration of the 20th century "Kilroy wos ere". When I was in Upnor castle I had noticed that a vandal had scratched onto the lead "John loves Julie 2012". How long does it take for vandalism to change to historical curio, I wonder? All of the staff at Eastgate House were extremely enthusiastic and helpful. The building is mentioned by Dickens in the Pickwick Papers and The Mystery of Edwin Drood.

The Swiss Chalet (not open to the public) is next to Eastgate house. You may remember that earlier in the book I said that whilst at school, English was not my forte. I positively hated reading my Dickens and I failed my English Literature O level. At the Swiss Chalet I was looking at the place where Charles Dickens wrote a number of his novels, including my now favourite, A Tale of Two Cities. Amazingly, the Swiss chalet was not built here but was moved from Dickens' other main place of work, Gads Hill in

Higham. It was originally made from a number of units which fitted together so dismantling and moving it to Rochester is not as bizarre as it seems. The flimsy orange chalet looked like it was in desperate need of renovation before it fell down.

I left Rochester, crossing the Medway via the dual carriageway and headed towards London. Keeping in a Dickens frame of mind I arrived in Higham. Gads Hill in Higham is where Dickens lived for part of his life. It now forms part of Gads Hill School, motto "First to thine own self be true". This is a much more ethereal motto compared to that of King's School in Rochester ("Learn or Leave"). Perhaps they are made of tougher stuff east of the Medway. Unfortunately, I could not get too close to the part where Dickens lived so had to satisfy myself with a walk down the hill, crossing the route of the old Thames and Medway canal, and then uphill to St Mary's church where Dicken's daughter was married. The church is now redundant, having been replaced by St John's which was built closer to Higham. Only one more literary mention of Dickens to come, I promise. Whilst visiting the church I passed by the sleepy Higham station. Looking eastwards, within one hundred yards of the station the railway line disappeared into a dirty white chalk tunnel.

The route of the Roman road should now have taken me to Dartford using the extremely busy A2 for part of the way. After my B2000 experience I copped out and got the train from Higham to Dartford with the proviso that I would then walk from Dartford to Marble Arch. As I had some time to wait before the arrival of my train I wandered the country lanes around Higham and was surprised to see four men wielding sticks and shouting. All became clear when a bird flew out of the undergrowth and another man shot it. This upset me. Am I a hypocrite, I do eat meat after all? Then again I don't kill animals in the name of sport. P.G. Wodehouse in "The Adventures of Sally" says

"The fascination of shooting as a sport depends almost wholly on whether you are at the right or wrong end of the gun."

Mark Levy, American Football coach born in 1925, put it totally in focus when he said

"When I was twelve, I went hunting with my father and we shot a bird. He was laying there and something struck me. Why do we call this fun to kill this creature who was as happy as I was when I woke up this morning?"

***

I am rather pleased that I took the train from Higham to Dartford rather than risk walking the section of Watling Street that is cunningly disguised as the A2. Just past Greenhithe station I caught a glimpse of the Queen Elizabeth Bridge. This was built for southbound traffic and supplements the northbound Dartford Tunnel. These are the only non-motorway sections of the M25. Seeing the bridge brought back happy memories of the many times I had traversed it whilst taking students from Cockermouth School to northern France. The trips always filled me with enthusiasm for my job. Seeing how these twelve year olds showed genuine interest and deep respect when visiting the First World War sites was very uplifting. At Thiepval in particular the students were keen to find their surnames on the giant Edwin Lutyen's war memorial. I appreciate that I was very lucky to have taught at Cockermouth, knowing that for many teachers at other schools their day to day working hours can be so stressful. Something else I now appreciated was how beautiful the bridge looked when viewed from a distance, the two tall central pillars acting as majestic sentinels for those moving upstream towards the capital.

When I arrived at Dartford station the area looked rather depressing. The station is hemmed in to the north by a building site (office blocks I presume) and a dual carriageway to the south. However, having crossed the bridge over the road, within two minutes I arrived at the pedestrianised High Street and things looked so different. I was pleased to note that the townspeople (workers and customers) had come out of the shopping centre to greet the intrepid traveller. As I was about to acknowledge my admiring hoards a uniformed person shouted, "Right, fire alarm over, you can re-enter the building". I sheepishly skulked past and went into the Royal Victoria and Bull, my hotel for the night.

It was built in 1703 and all rooms were undergoing a major refurbishment (not the first since 1703 I assume). In the past it had been a cattle market and corn exchange. I was told that I would be in Jane Bennett's room. Gallantly, I said that there was no need to throw her out on my account. One of the builders kindly led me past the corridor that had bedrooms still being refurbished and took me to the section of the hotel that had rather plush rooms. Mine had "Jane Bennett" written on the door. I then noticed that the other rooms had the names of the rest of the Bennett sisters on. Ah, it all became clear now. Someone was a fan of Pride and Prejudice. Coincidentally, Jane Austen started writing the novel after staying at Goodnestone Park which was less than three miles from the hotel I stayed at in Littlebourne. There was no "Jane Austen slept here" plaque at my hotel in Dartford so I am not too sure what the connection is. I ate my dinner at the hotel and opted for what was billed as a local dish; pie, mash and liquor. It was most enjoyable. My research showed that this was a favourite meal in the Southeast of England with many Eel and Pie shops having at one time dotted the landscape. Thank goodness there was no eel in the pie I ate. I was intrigued as to what the liquor was made from. Beer or whisky maybe? And then I found the answer. Liquor is a mucus coloured gravy made from parsley and stock that comes from boiling eels.

My route now took me on a very straight course, from Dartford to Blackheath. For all but a tiny section I passed only shops and houses with little or no greenery. I made rapid progress through Crayford, Bexleyheath and Welling. Just past Welling I started a steady climb up the A207. This went on for about a mile and at the top I was sweating profusely. I had a great view downhill towards Blackheath. I looked at the road sign and it said "Shooters Hill", the road that was once notorious as a place where highwaymen and murderers lurked.

And now, as promised, my last literary reference to Charles Dickens. My favourite Dickens novel, A Tale of Two Cities, starts with passengers on the Dover Mail coach being asked to get out so that the horses could pull the carriage up Shooters Hill. They were all on their guard for highwaymen. It has been suggested that at the time the novel was set there was no such thing as the Dover Mail coach, mail having been transported using post boys on horseback. What I didn't realise was that this place is also mentioned in Byron's Don Juan. At the bottom of the hill the road crossed the South Circular Road and got noticeably busier.

***

Half a mile further on I came to a sign for Charlton Lido. I have three childhood memories of swimming baths. At the age of thirteen I learnt to swim at Sharston baths in south Manchester. After each lesson I would get a Tunnocks caramel wafer at the shop and chew this on my way home. I still enjoy Tunnocks, both the wafers and their wagon wheels. Once I went to the baths and I was the only person in the pool. It was so cold that I could not catch my breath. The baths always struggled to make ends meet so it came as no surprise when demolition took place and an office block was put up instead.

Another place I remember was Castle Mill outdoor pool near Styal in Cheshire. I recall hanging onto the side rail at the shallow end screaming for dear life as my Dad tried to drag me into the water. How I must have embarrassed him. I think my fear of water arose from the time I went to Chorlton baths in Manchester. Whilst I stood at the shallow end, my uncle told me to jump in and reassured me that he would catch me. Being a trusting four year old I did as he said. Unfortunately, he neither caught me nor pulled me to the side. Then again, this was the same uncle who told the kids to go and play on the motorway when we were playing noisily in the house. He never did have children.

Dad had a nifty trick of running along the diving board, jumping up, landing back down on the end of the board on his bottom and then flipping into the water. For at least the last ten years of his life Dad was blind and I am grateful for the memories of him in his prime. He used to love playing football and cricket with us and also played in the police cricket team. On one occasion he let me tag along to one of the matches. As we waited at the bus stop (car ownership was rare in the late fifties) another player stopped and gave us a lift on his motorbike. It was the one and only time I have ever ridden in a sidecar; very exciting. Whilst the match was progressing I rummaged in the pavilion and found what I thought was a face protector. Putting it on, I proudly walked outside to the amusement of all the players. Dad shouted to me to take it off. I had embarrassed him again. How did I know that the boxes, as they are called, are designed to protect the more tender parts of a man's anatomy.

The biggest dragonflies I have ever seen used to fly over the pool at Castle Mill. They put the fear of God in me. Sadly, it had to make way for the second runway at Manchester Airport. As a child living in Baguley I used to have wonderful family walks and cycle rides in the quiet country lanes, all of which slowly disappeared as the expansion of the airport took place.

Another abiding memory of swimming baths is not of my childhood but my daughter Claire's. One of my treats was to spend Sunday mornings with her at Horwich baths and we would spend an age in the parent and child pool. The water was warm and I was the shark, chasing Claire up and down the pool. These sessions helped to ease the stresses of my job and get me mentally prepared for the week ahead.

***

Charlton Lido is part of a private sports centre but is open to the public. After my hot slog up Shooters Hill I was ready for a cooling swim. I was the only person in the pool. Thankfully, despite it being outdoors, it felt like the pool was heated. After a relaxing half hour I dressed and walked on to Blackheath, bought a caramel wafer and a wagon wheel and ate them both whilst sitting in Batley Park.

Blackheath is only known to me from my avid reading of the Sherlock Holmes cannon. I have read all of the Holmes stories, many times over, both in book and Kindle versions. I even have all the stories in audio book format on my iPod. In the Norwood Builder, Holmes tells Inspector Lestrade "You should go to Blackheath first". In the Sussex Vampire reference is made to Watson having played rugby for Blackheath. However, Blackheath has more to offer than passing references by Conan Doyle. In 1381 and then in 1450, two revolts began with the gathering of rebels at Blackheath.

I was taught at school about the Peasants Revolt (1381) led by Wat Tyler but had not heard of Jack Cade (1450). The first of these was caused by the introduction of a poll tax, which was levied against all people, rich or poor. In addition conditions of the poor and their treatment as serfs were issues that resulted in Tyler leading a march into London. Negotiations with Richard II seemed to be resulting in concessions for the demonstrators. For some reason the meeting took a turn for the worse, Tyler stabbed the Lord Mayor of London which resulted in Tyler then being stabbed and killed. He was later beheaded and his head put on a pole on London Bridge. After the death of their leader, the demonstrators quickly dispersed and never received any concessions from the king. The poll tax (community charge) dissent in the late 20th century was more productive as it resulted in an eventual U-turn by the "The lady's not for turning" prime minister, Margaret Thatcher.

Jack Cade's rebellion over a hundred years after the Peasants Revolt was against the rule of Henry VI, who was seen as a weak and corrupt king by many. Cade wanted the corruption to end and the removal of those advisors to the king who were seen as traitors and symbols of that corruption. On their arrival in London the rebels could not be kept under control and started looting. Any sympathy the locals may have had was quickly changed to fear and aggression. Cade's men were defeated in a battle near London Bridge and driven out of the city. Eventually he was captured following a struggle during which he received fatal wounds. Whilst on the way back to London to stand trial for treason Cade died.

Having then walked the short distance from Blackheath to Greenwich Park, I booked into a hotel and had an early night. This would be the only place that I stayed on my road trip that was part of a major budget hotel chain. The next morning I had a somewhat surreal experience whilst trying to get my breakfast. To save the hotel any embarrassment I will not mention it by name but call it, let's say for the sake of argument, the Gravel Lodge in Greenwich. Going into the breakfast room at 09.45 (fifteen minutes before breakfast finishes) I obediently waited at a large sign that said "Wait here to be seated". Nobody was having breakfast and there was no-one in Reception. I waited for five minutes. A man came out from the kitchen, looked at me, cleared a table and went back into the kitchen. After a further five minutes he came out, looked at me, put some clean plates out and went back into the kitchen. Five minutes later he came back out, looked at me and shouted across the room, "Sorry mate, we stop serving breakfast at ten". And that was it. I dropped my key at reception (still no-one to be seen) and walked up to the Royal Greenwich Observatory. Before going in I had a pot of tea and a slice of cake at their café.

From the café I walked round to the entrance to the Observatory and stopped to admire the view, and some view it was. I could see across Greenwich Park towards the National Maritime Museum and Queens House and across the Thames to Canary Wharf and the Millennium Dome. It was stunning. From this point the Romans would have seen nothing but river and marshland. I could see the skyscrapers of the modern banking district. My name for the place is Claustrophobia.

As someone whose twin interests are Science and History I was now in my element. The busiest part of the Observatory was the meridian line. Numerous people were crowding around the line having their pictures taken, standing at the point on the line depicting their country of origin. This was okay by me as it meant that the real guts of the museum were less busy. Armed with a free audio tour gadget, I plugged in my earphones and spent the next couple of hours wallowing in the experience. Seeing the actual clocks that John Harrison built to help mariners calculate longitude accurately was amazing. His inventions helped to make long sea journeys safer in terms of ships actually getting to the right place rather than a few miles off course. Ten miles off course may not sound much but in an ocean of little but water, missing land could be a matter of life and death. The audio guide explained machines and timelines in an easy to follow and interesting manner. The part of the museum devoted to exploration of the stars was no less enthralling. The Royal

Observatory is definitely now in my top three museums (along with the Natural History and Imperial War museums).

I wandered down the hill, through the park and into the National Maritime Museum (NMM). This is one of the many free museums around the country. We are so lucky to have this access. In austere times I can see this free entry being removed. Speaking personally, I would not begrudge paying an entry fee to ensure that we can have access to our many splendid museums. The NMM was okay. However, having been spoilt in the Royal Observatory, in comparison it was just okay. What did fascinate me though was the special exhibition that was on. Entry to the "Franklin, Death in the Ice" exhibition was not free, but it was well worth the fee. Franklin was someone that I had never heard of. In 1845 he captained two ships, HMS Erebus and HMS Terror, and went in search of the northwest passage (a hoped for northerly route from the Atlantic to the Pacific that would take many weeks off the existing routes). All contact was lost for a number of years. The last known position of the ships placed them to the north of Canada. Eventually human remains were found and then only recently the ships were discovered, sunk in shallow water. It is believed that the ships got stuck in the ice for up to three years and at some point the crews tried to find a way across the icy landscape. Human and non-human remains from the expedition have been found over a wide area. Analysis of them has proved inconclusive so far. The burning question seems to be, why did they abandon the ships when there was plenty of food and other provisions still on board? The exhibition was sombre but excellent.

Whilst in the exhibition I noticed one small piece of information. I did say that there would be no more literary references to Dickens. However, I include the following quote from him as it does not relate to any of his novels. Without any evidence to back up his statement he says in Household Words on 2nd December 1854.

> *"No man can with any show of reason undertake to affirm that the sad remnants of Franklin's gallant band were not set upon and slain by Inuits themselves".*

Is this an indication of racism from the great man? I leave the reader to judge. After the NMM I wandered across the road to see Cutty Sark. I did not go on board as I had seen one just like it in Chatham. I then went southwest and then westwards and got to Old Kent Road, the name of Watling Street in this part of London.

Later that day I would be walking through Mayfair to get to Marble Arch so I thought that a bit of research on the board game Monopoly was in order. Having been brought up on this classic London based game I assumed that the Americans had usurped it to make their own New York version. I had got things completely the wrong way round. The game was invented in 1903 by Elizabeth Maggie to demonstrate the negative aspects of monopolies. She called it the Landlord's Game. Parker Brothers bought the copyright in 1934, changed the name to Monopoly and two years later licenced the game for sale outside the US. I love the next part of the story. In 1941 the British Secret Service asked John Waddington to devise a version of the game that could be sent to prisoners of war in Germany. Maps, compasses and real money were hidden inside these games.

Talking of board games, my all-time favourite was Risk. Many sleepless nights were spent with members of the family (siblings and in-laws) trying to out manoeuvre one another, each vying to achieve world domination. After years of trying, my sister Joy eventually won a game at the end of a particularly exhausting night. To mark this unbelievable occasion the rest of us decided to retire permanently from the game. She says that it was the shock of losing to her that put us off playing Risk again. My other favourite was Cluedo, more cerebral than Risk, but no less competitive. Even now I spend long hours playing games with members of the family, often until the early hours. On one memorable occasion I played table football against Stuart, using two penny pieces for players and a penny for the ball. Sausage rolls doubled up as goalposts, and very tasty they were too. I am not a very competitive person until it comes to board games, whether playing solo or in a team, and I made sure that I ate more than my share of goalposts.

Old Kent Road was the typical unattractive urban collection of houses, businesses, super stores and traffic. Why did it warrant the notoriety of being the cheapest property on the Monopoly board (£100 with rental of £2 if an opponent lands on it)? Okay, I admit that it is not quite as pretty as Mayfair (£400 with rental of £50) which is bordered on one side by Hyde Park. Old Kent Road is the only property from South London featured in the game. From here I veered slightly west. I did this for two reasons; firstly to visit the Imperial War Museum and secondly because that is what the Romans did.

The Imperial War Museum (yet again free entry) does not glorify war but remembers the sacrifices that service personnel and civilians undergo during conflicts. As with my visits to the war graves in France, the Museum never fails to move me. There is no denying that some of the hardware and munitions on display are most impressive, but it is the personal stories that linger most in one's memory. The Holocaust Exhibition pulls no punches and can be too overwhelming for some visitors. However, it is a story that needs to be told and remembered so people understand the horrors that can be done when people turn a blind eye. Eyes were conveniently turned at the start of the 20th century during the second Boer War. The first ever concentration camps were set up and tens of thousands of men, women and children died in them. These camps were set up by the British.

***

The Roman road route from Rochester to Greenwich, a straight north westerly line, had been relatively easy to follow and carrying on in this direction to Marble Arch would then have lead me to cross the Thames somewhere between Westminster and Waterloo bridges. However, as mentioned previously, I had to go southwest from Greenwich to get to Old Kent Road before turning north-west again. Margary (page 52) writes,

> "It is interesting to note that this long alignment, laid out from Swanscombe, does, in fact, point directly to Westminster, the site of the traditional ford said to have been the earlier crossing-place of the Thames before the construction of London Bridge. However, it would not have been possible for Watling Street to have been continued straight on along this line owing to the curve of the river at Greenwich and the marshy ground beyond".

The defeated Britons had crossed the Thames further downstream, perhaps near Gravesend. They would have understood the vagaries of the tidal nature of the Thames and when and where mud flats would appear. The Romans needed a reliable crossing place and so had aimed for a ford (close to modern day Westminster Bridge) which their spies had no doubt scouted out previously. They then set up a fortified camp on the north side of the river.

They built a bridge out of wood where London Bridge now stands, eventually replacing it by a stone structure. In their early bridges, stone blocks were held together by iron clamps. Then the Romans started to use concrete in the 2nd century AD (yes, it also surprised me that concrete is not a modern invention). They were also the first to identify the strength that arches brought to structures that spanned waterways and valleys. Some of their aqueducts and bridges bear testimony to the Romans' expertise in civil engineering projects.

The Roman army caught its breath whilst Plautius awaited Claudius and his elephants. They were then ready for the final push against the Catuvellauni at Colchester.

I didn't have time to catch my breath as time was short. Crossing the Thames by the modern day Westminster Bridge I made my way to Marble Arch. It was a most enjoyable stroll, snaking my way there using paths in St James Park, Green Park and Hyde Park. I wandered past the Houses of Parliament and Buckingham Palace too. Planners in London should be congratulated for the number of quite marvellous parks, both large and small, that are dotted throughout the metropolis. Resisting the temptation to have a dip in the Serpentine, I stopped at Speakers Corner but no-one was speaking so moved on. I then walked along the north side of Hyde Park and spent the night near Queensway tube station at a typically cheapish and cheerless hotel (to be referred to as C and C hereon in).

Hotels in London seem to have the ability to cram a shower and toilet into as small a space as possible. Without going into too much detail, when sitting down in the little boy's room, I needed to keep the door open so as to get my knees to fit. Despite the lack of space, the room managed to shoe horn in a bed, wardrobe, TV, bedside table, me and my extra-large rucksack. At least there was no chance of falling out of the narrow bed when turning over during the night; lying on my left side meant my nose was squashed against the wall and on the right side against the bedside table with the kettle on. Another plus was that there was no need to get out of bed when turning lights on and off or making a brew. Perhaps Roman houses had more spacious rooms than the average London hotel.

5 LONDON (LONDINIUM)

Route: Margary The London Area (pages 53-59).

Having originally crossed the Thames via Westminster Bridge, close to the ford that the Romans would have used when they first traversed the river, I now made my way from my hotel (close to Marble Arch) to the site of the permanent bridge that the Romans built. London Bridge marks the riverside entry point to the walled town that was established on the north bank of the Thames. The exact line, depth and tidal reach of the river would have been different to the present waterway. Suffice to say that two thousand years ago it was navigable from here to the Thames estuary and beyond. In addition, the river Fleet (running south to the Thames just west of the Roman city wall) and the river Walbrook (southwards through the centre of the city and providing fresh drinking water) no longer exist.

My plan was to wander through Londinium; start at London Bridge, go west along the Thames, north via Ludgate and Newgate, east near Cripplegate and Bishopsgate, south via Aldgate and the Tower of London and then west along the Thames back to London Bridge. The area I have described follows the old wall of the Roman city and pretty much encompasses the modern day City of London. Southwark, on the opposite bank of the river was a marshy area unsuitable for urban development.

The geographical area of London equivalent to that enclosed by the Roman wall has had a wax and wane existence. A small settlement was thought to exist there prior to the Roman occupation. The Roman site must have been present by the middle of the 1st century as it is recorded that it was sacked during the Iceni revolt of AD60-61. Within a hundred years it became the largest Roman settlement when it replaced Colchester as the administrative capital. When the Romans left Britain in AD410, Londinium and the area inside the walls was abandoned and eventually became almost derelict. The Saxons initially chose to develop their settlement, called Londenwic, further west, close to the Strand. Alfred the Great, needing to have towns that could be readily defended from attack by the Danes, redeveloped the area within the walls and the place became known as Lundenburh. Throughout attacks by the Vikings and Normans it expanded steadily to what we see today. It would appear that the line of the Roman wall has been the unofficial boundary for the city ever since the wall was built. Currently almost 10,000 people live within the area that was once enclosed by the wall, but during the day commuters to the district swell this number thirty times to over 300,000; finance, insurance and legal professions accounting for most of these. Tourists, including me, increase this number substantially.

I crossed the busy roads and sidestepped through the streets like a demented fly half in a game of rugby (or for those thousands of people from the ex-colony who buy this book, a manic running back in a game of American Football). Were all 300,000 plus people having a lunchtime stroll? I felt that I was taking my life in my hands. A few years previously, traffic and pedestrians would have been the least of my worries. Lindsay Allason-Jones in her book "Women in Roman Britain" (page 77) comments about sewerage systems in towns. She says that,

> *"The sewers, like the aqueducts, were often open or built very close to the surface, leading to unpleasant smells and the spread of disease, while their content invariably emptied into the nearest river or stream on which another community might rely for its water supply. Dysentery, diarrhoea and internal parasites were rife, as were the*

other diseases of overcrowding and pollution: London, for example, may have been decimated by plague in the second century."

Moving from a rural to an urban environment, with its perceived increase in convenience and sophistication, may have appealed to swathes of the populace but it would also have had a detrimental effect on health. After the Romans left these shores London was visited on numerous occasions by plague and disease. It wasn't just the well documented Black Death of 1348 or the Great Plague of 1665 that Londoners had to cope with. In between those dates around 40 outbreaks occurred, killing 20 percent of the population each time.

Closely packed communities were more liable to spread of disease even without allowing for poor sanitary arrangements. Raw sewage floating down the Thames helped make up the toxic soup that included plague, smallpox, syphilis, typhus and malaria. Victorian London during the Industrial Revolution added cholera and scarlet fever to the long list of diseases that could affect residents and visitors to the capital. It was as late as 1854 that John Snow demonstrated a link between contaminated drinking water and illness but it took another thirty years for his ideas to be widely accepted. And let's not forget that other killer that lasted until the mid-1950s; smog, a deadly mixture of smoke particles and fog. In December 1952 the Great Smog, as it was called, lasted for five days. It was estimated to be the worst air pollution event in the history of these islands and at least 4,000 and perhaps as many as 12,000 deaths in London have been attributed to it. The Clean Air Act of 1956 came about as a consequence of this tragedy. I have childhood memories of these so called pea soupers in Manchester. On one occasion we had been visiting my grandparents in Levenshulme and waited in Piccadilly for a bus back to Baguley. The smog was so thick that you could not see the number on the bus even when it had arrived at the stop. The vehicle travelled at walking pace for three miles and then as if by magic the smog lifted. Another time I remember my Dad returning home one morning from night duty as a policeman in Manchester city centre. He blew his nose in his handkerchief and it was black.

If disease didn't get you then the risk of fire may well have. When was the Great Fire of London? We think of that happening in 1666. The fire raged for three nights and yet only six people are officially recorded as having died. This is probably an understatement as deaths of working class people were not recorded. Much of the medieval city was destroyed. The fire was allegedly started by accident in a bakery. The Worshipful Company of Bakers made an apology to the Lord Mayor of London. However, this admission did not nullify any potential insurance claims as it was made in 1986, only 320 years too late. Thatched roofs were banned in the city following the fire. London has suffered other great fires where much of the city was destroyed. During the Roman occupation in AD60 (during Boudicca's revolt) and AD122 (an accident) few buildings were left unscathed. There were at least another dozen serious fires before the one in 1666. So, we should really call that one a great fire of London and not The etc.

Between September 1940 and May 1941 Londoners underwent continuous risk of death during the Second World War blitz from Nazi bombers, resulting in over 40,000 deaths and hundreds of thousands of houses destroyed. In the latter stages of that war fire and destruction again visited the capital when Hitler's new weapons, the V1 cruise missile and V2 ballistic rocket (the V stands for vergeltungswaffen, reprisal weapon) were aimed indiscriminatingly at London. Over 6,000 people died. These two were more sinister weapons as there was no time to seek safety in underground shelters. Then again the shelters were not without their dangers. In 1943 at Bethnal Green tube station 173 people were crushed to death after panic set in when a woman fell down the stairs.

So, you managed to avoid catching any nasty bugs, being burnt to a crisp or blown to smithereens. Hey ho, you could have ended up being a crime statistic. Luckily, there has been a police presence in one form or another in the city of London since Roman times. In later years the area was policed by the Bow Street Runners (1748-1829), the first professional police force in Britain. Thereafter it became the responsibility of the City of London Police, sometimes known as "bobbies" or "peelers", named after its founder Sir Robert Peel. They cover an area closely fitting that which was enclosed by the Roman wall. The Metropolitan Police are a different organisation. Other less complementary nicknames for the police do exist. However, with regard to those I invoke my right to remain silent.

* * *

With that lucky to be alive feeling I elbowed my way through a roughly circular route around the old Roman town, starting at London Bridge. The current bridge is fairly new. In 1968 the 19th century granite bridge was bought by an American for almost $2.5 million, dismantled and shipped to the USA and reconstructed in Lake Havasu in Arizona. Sadly, it is an urban myth that the purchaser thought he was buying the iconic Tower Bridge and was conned into buying the bland one he ended up with.

The first bridge that the Romans built across the Thames would have been a temporary structure made of timber. As they expanded their provincial capital they created something more substantial out of stone. Whilst in The Museum of London I came across a mock-up of what the original wooden bridge may have looked like (see below). The modern bridge gives a somewhat different perspective as it looks towards the skyscrapers of the business district.

From the bridge the first thing of note that I came across was Sir Christopher Wren's Monument to the Great Fire of London; talk about rubbing salt into the wounds of the Worshipful Company of Bakers. It was huge and had a viewing platform at the top. I seemed to be the only person in London who was looking at it. In comparison to Nelson's Column it obviously is not on many people's list of must see places.

Next on my list of must see places was the Millennium Bridge. This footbridge was built to celebrate the year 2000 along with that wonderful white elephant known as the Millennium Dome. How come the Welsh managed to build a superb stadium to celebrate the occasion yet the English thought it proper to build an upturned wok and a footbridge that was too dangerous for people to walk across? I kid you not. Having taken two years to be built, the footbridge had to be closed on its grand opening day as it induced something akin to seasickness; it was called the wobbly bridge. Then it was opened for limited access (weight and height restrictions?) for two days and soon after closed for two years. I can confirm that the wobble has been eliminated.

Walking northwards along the footbridge I got a great view of the dome of St Paul's cathedral. Perhaps this was why the bridge was built here. Once inside, St Paul's seemed small compared to Canterbury cathedral, yet it is classed as the second largest church in the country (Liverpool being number one). However, it does have the dome which you can walk up to. A church has been on this site since AD604 and has been rebuilt on a number of occasions due to fire damage. What we see today is the result of the Great Fire of London in 1666. Christopher Wren redesigned the cathedral with its world famous dome. This place of worship has witnessed the funerals of many national heroes including Horatio Nelson, the Duke of Wellington, Winston Churchill and Margaret Thatcher (hero or anti-hero depending on your politics). The cathedral's finest hour came about the same time as Churchill talked about the country's finest hour. During the blitz in WW2, the dome stood proud, echoing the indomitable spirit of the Londoners who endured the bombing.

I wandered along to the Old Bailey, hoping to see barristers in wig and gown rushing hither and thither. No luck, just bog standard commuters. I craned my neck skywards to get a sight of the statue on top of the Old Bailey; blindfolded, with sword in one hand and the scales of justice in the other. Now don't get me wrong, I do understand the symbolism, but I'd be rather wary of a blindfolded person coming towards me wielding a huge sword in one hand and swinging a load of heavy metal in the other. Then again, they would have been arrested for carrying offensive weapons.

On my way from the Old Bailey to the Museum of London I seemed to be hemmed in on all sides by towering masses of glass and concrete. Ahead of me was the banking district. I could imagine that within these edifices, thousands of commuters were plying their trade; faceless generators of cash for the global capitalists. Here, and not in Westminster or Whitehall, was the decision making hub of the nation. Government policies have to consider their impact on the financial markets. It is said that power corrupts and the power that money creates brings the greatest corruption. Many nations, including this one, were brought to their knees by the global banking scandal that was driven by immense greed. Both the right and left of the political spectrum chose to ignore such avarice. Hopefully, controls are in place to avoid another financial crisis but I somehow doubt it. Everyone wants to get on the gravy train.

Passing through the stifling streets I suddenly came upon an oasis of calm, Christchurch Grey Friars Garden. Here a few tourists and cyclists were catching their breath on the benches that surrounded the place. I joined them and, amazingly, the cacophony from the streets seemed to disappear and I could hear birdsong. The buildings that had only seconds ago appeared so threatening were now just an irrelevant backdrop to my peace of mind. I wandered slowly around the garden and then made my way to the Museum of London.

I wanted to see the Roman exhibition in the museum. Thirty primary school children had the same idea too. It was most enjoyable watching them looking at the exhibits and filling in answers on their worksheets. Among the exhibits was a full scale mock-up of a Roman living room, and rather comfortable and roomy it looked too with settee and chairs and no TV (see below). I must admit that I am not a great television watcher, apart from history programmes and rugby. Oh, and endless repeats of the American detective series, Columbo. I think I am turning into my Mum as she is a fan too.

The Museum had far more to offer than just artefacts and scale models depicting Londinium. Here was a potted history of the nation's capital and it was done in a most informative way. In one area I sat watching old black and white children's programmes from the late fifties and early sixties. I was transported back to my infancy. Memories flashed before my eyes; Andy Pandy, the Wooden Tops, Bill and Ben the Flowerpot Men. I had total recall, being able to sing along (quietly) as each of my childhood favourites started. This was the age of innocence when children didn't worry that you could see the strings of the puppets, or that Bill and Ben spoke in a totally unintelligible language. In my reverie I thought back to my daughter's early childhood and how we used to love sitting together, watching her favourite programmes: Rosie and Jim, Tots TV and a series whose name I cannot recall featuring characters called Mossop and Glossop. Then it struck me - there was no violence in any of these programmes, both from mine or my daughter's eras. Does the age of innocence end when we are alerted to the violence around us?

Three hours went by in the Museum of London. Whilst there I got a good view of part of the Roman wall of the city.

In addition, I read that part of the Roman amphitheatre had been unearthed when the Guildhall was being redeveloped. In the basement of the Guildhall Art Gallery were the remains of the amphitheatre. So I made an unscheduled stop (it was in the right direction anyway). The Guildhall is the administrative centre for the City of London (not to be confused with Greater London's City Hall). The fifteenth century building along with its newer additions enclose a large courtyard that had been used as what looked like a French market on the day I visited. In the art gallery I made my way to the amphitheatre. All that remains are a few nondescript piles of stones.

I listened in on a talk that was being given as part of a seminar and was pleasantly surprised to find that I understood quite lot of what was being said. My book research had broadened my knowledge.

Time was marching on so I marched on towards the Roman Wall and the Tower of London. Outside of its context the wall looked just like an old ruined wall, which is exactly what it is. The Tower on the other hand is an impressively eye catching building steeped in history. The current series of buildings date back to Norman times. Their grandeur and strategic positioning overlooking the entrance to the city would have sent a strong message to would be invaders from the sea, "Don't mess with us, matey". As well as housing the Crown Jewels, the Tower has been used to house a number of well-known historical figures prior to release (Elizabeth I before she became queen), execution (Walter Raleigh, Anne Boleyn and Lady Jane Grey) or unexplained disappearance (Richard III's alleged murder of the "Princes in the Tower"). Guy Fawkes was tortured in the Tower before his admission of guilt and execution. It is also a handy place to view Tower Bridge from.

My final stop on the way back towards London Bridge was Billingsgate Roman house and baths. This is part of the Museum of London and, like so many of the country's museums, is free of charge. As you approach it there is no hint of what lies beneath the buildings. These 2nd and 3rd century remains were first uncovered in 1848 when the Coal Exchange was built and the remaining parts unearthed when the Coal Exchange was demolished in the late 1960's. It is great that London has such a regard for its heritage. When any new building work takes place, archaeologists are firstly given the opportunity to investigate the site. When built the house would have been positioned at a prime location, with the river running past it.

And then I was back where I started from six hours earlier. Once I had completed my circuit it struck home how small the Roman city of Londinium (and the current City of London) actually was. No wonder this area is called the Square Mile. Of course, there would have been many dwellings and businesses outside the city walls, including south of the river. I had only been looking at the area enclosed by a defensive wall. Around 60,000 people lived in the vicinity in Roman times.

***

During my stroll around this part of London it was obvious that much money has been invested. It is a constant moan of northerners that an inordinate amount of investment in infrastructure and jobs has gone into the southeast. During pipe laying operations in London, a Roman road was unearthed for a considerable length. Commenting on the construction at this point Margary (page 55) says,

"It was of very solid construction, consisting of one foot of rammed gravel with one foot of carefully laid large nodular flints set in lime grouting upon it, with a kerb wall of gravel concrete to hold the edges of the road. This is Roman road construction at its best, and is reasonable enough upon such an important highway."

It seems that even in those days, Londinium got preferential treatment compared to the rest of the country. Okay, so I'm a northern moaner.

Another thing that struck me (apart from what a lot of glass has been used to build London's more modern buildings) was the wonderful, vibrant cosmopolitan feel about the place. It would have been like that in Roman times too. At least 40,000 foreign soldiers arrived in AD43. Throughout the 400 years of occupation there would have been a constant movement from and to continental Europe.

Whereas the legionaries were mostly Roman citizens from Italy, the auxiliaries came from provinces far and wide. Most came from Gaul, the Rhineland and Spain and they would have spoken a Celtic language similar to the Britons. Others came from further afield (modern day Iran, Africa and the Danube to name but a few). As the Romans marched inland then some of the Britons would have followed too (willingly for trade or unwillingly as slaves). Barry Cunliffe cites the case of a woman's tombstone from Hadrian's Wall. Regina was from the Catuvellauni in Hertfordshire who became a slave. She was freed and married Barates, from Palmyra close to the Syrian Desert. Her tombstone was inscribed in both Latin and Palmyrene.

Reflecting the cultural diversity, dining out in London is a truly eclectic experience. Recipes from every continent can be had, be it gourmet or fast food. The Romans too didn't want simple fare. In the 1st century AD Apicius, their equivalent of Delia Smith, wrote a book on sauces and contributed to an early collection of recipes called "The Art of Cooking". Whereas there are copious lists of ingredients, two minor details seem to be missing; quantities and cooking temperatures. Lindsay Allason-Jones (page 95) says,

> *"There seems to have been a dislike for the plain taste of meat, fish or vegetables, and herbs, spices and sauces were used extensively. This may have been due to the difficulty of storing fresh food".*

My parents were born in India and I was brought up on curries. Mum used to say that the spices helped to preserve the food as well as add delicious flavours. Getting us used to the spices was a rites of passage, copied by each of my siblings in turn. As soon as we were weened we had our first taste of Indian food, dhal and rice. The dhal was basically split red lentils with a little sugar, a pinch of salt, turmeric and ginger boiled with water (one cup of lentils, two of water) until it became a thick sauce. After a couple of years we were allowed to have a curried potato with the dhal. Eventually we were given a plate of curry and rice, with a portion of dhal on the side. How grown up I felt sitting down with my plate of curry, listening to the long and exciting tales of life in India told by my parents and grandparents. My Dad never referred to India by name, always calling it "out there". My favourite curry was kofta curry; the meatballs that my Nana used to make were so succulent and spicy. Strangely, she never ate curry herself. Even now I regularly make lentil curry (without the sugar) and occasionally one of my childhood favourites, pilchard curry.

Should you be tempted by "The Art of Cooking", Allason-Jones goes on to mention some of the more exotic recipes, including testicles of capon, sow's udders, lights of hare and entrails of fish. I remember enjoying a plate of sweetbreads once only to be told that they came from the thymus or pancreas of calf. On hindsight, it was offal. Evidence of meat and fish bones uncovered during excavations disproves the popular myth that Romano Britons were mainly vegetarian. Also, it was not just the wealthy who ate meat. So, dining in Londinium would have been a gourmet's delight. Maybe they had their equivalent of pie, mash and liquor too.

Thankfully, one thing that did appear to be missing from the streets that I walked along was dog mess. When I went to Paris a while ago, to see a Genesis concert, I christened the place Dog Poo City. Sadly, some of the streets in Penrith are getting the same way. Londinium would have had its share of excrement. Romans were great lovers of pets (dogs, cats and birds) and there would have been a lot of carts trundling through the streets. The arrival of Claudius' elephants would obviously have temporarily increased the volume of manure. AD43 would have been a good year for the roses in Britannia. Incidentally, roses were grown throughout the Roman Empire, being used in medicines, as confetti and in perfumes. They were also grown for their aesthetic beauty with public rose gardens being built in Rome and elsewhere.

I made my way to my hotel (cheapish and cheerless again) in Aldgate in readiness for my detour to Colchester. Aldgate would have been the exit point for Plautius's army on their march east to the Catuvellauni capital. Rather than take advantage of the gastronomic delights that were available I popped into a Tesco local and bought a sandwich and a couple of cans of beer and had them in my tiny room. As I ate and drank my Tesco dinner I wondered how the invading army got its sustenance without the benefit of open-all-hours corner shops. To be honest, I hadn't a clue and realised that more research was going to have to be undertaken to answer that one. But it was now time to retire for the night, so I put that question to bed until chapter eight.

In the morning I awoke to a crisp frost. It was bitterly cold. The clocks had recently gone back an hour and the evenings were getting dark very early. Reluctantly, I had to admit that my campaign season was over for the year. The Romans had a campaign season too. In fact, a major contributory factor in Julius Caesar's failed invasion in 55BC had been that he had set out too late. I would have to wait until the spring to continue my road trip, firstly to Colchester and then north up Ermine Street to York. To be fair, I had been blessed so far with unseasonably pleasant autumnal weather, apart from that day when I walked in the teeming, driving rain from Faversham to Rainham. It should have been a three hour train journey from Euston to Penrith to get me back to my winter quarters and ready for four months hibernation. Unfortunately, due to severe rainstorms in Lancashire and flooding of the track, the train terminated at Preston and I had to complete my journey by bus. I got home over three hours late. I felt sorry for those who had to get a bus all the way to Glasgow, not because they were going to Glasgow, you understand. Those poor passengers would have added an extra six hours to their journey time, allowing for the long queues for the buses at Preston and then the relatively slow drive north.

6 DETOUR – LONDON TO COLCHESTER

Route: London to Chelmsford Margary 3a (pages 246-247).

Route: Chelmsford to Colchester Margary 3b (pages 247-250).

With the spring came a renewed spring in my step. My campaign season was about to start again. Rather than start my journey north along Ermine Street, following the Ninth Legion's conquest trail, I had decided to take a detour before returning back to the original route. Basically, I was looking to follow in the footsteps of giants. If you remember (and if not, why not?), Aulus Plautius reached London during the conquest and then waited for Claudius to arrive before pushing on to defeat the Catuvellauni at Colchester.

Colchester would have been seen as a prize worth striving for. Patricia Southern in "Roman Britain a New History 55BC-AD450" (page 30) says,

> *"By the time of the Claudian invasion, the tribes of south Britain had established centralised settlements, known to the Romans as oppida, the most important one being at Colchester, with other settlements at Verulamium (St Albans) and Silchester. The inhabitants of these settlements established mints and issued their own coins."*

Capturing Colchester would not only have shattered local morale but also sent a powerful message to other tribes.

Claudius had some excess baggage. Not only did he bring siege machines with him but also up to 38 elephants. These must have really put the fear of the gods in the tribesmen. And I was going to follow these giants.

Latin joke: Where did the Romans display their huge creatures? In the circus maximus of course.

Talking of the circus maximus, when in Rome I visited it with my daughter Claire and noted that it was very long, straight and flat (but not boring) with tight curves. In films about ancient Rome, when a chariot race is filmed the race track always appears to be like a motor bike speedway track; lots of curves and short straight sections. In practice the circus maximus was designed to give chariots the opportunity to get into top gear and really motor along. Can you talk about chariots motoring along? Then again, we talk about a car having such and such a horsepower engine and cars motor along. My detour seems to have taken a detour of its own. Back to Aldgate.

***

I arrived at Aldgate via train and tube from Penrith by late morning. To get to my overnight stop in Stratford would take no more than five miles. Zigzagging my way along the streets I made my way from Aldgate to Bethnal Green. No traces of a Roman road link these two. Margary says (page 56),

> *"The Colchester Road. This, the main artery to the chief tribal capital and to East Anglia, must have been one of the earliest highways, and its course east of Stratford is well represented by the present roads. The Lea valley was crossed at Old Ford, about half a mile to the north of Bow Bridge, which is a much later crossing, and remains of Roman masonry have been found there, near Iceland Wharf. From this point a road must have gone direct to Aldgate and the bridge, although no traces have been found outside the city."*

Bethnal Green is anything but green nowadays. However, it used to be an agricultural area that provided fresh produce for London. As mentioned in the previous chapter, the local tube station was the place where 173 people died in the crush following the fall on the stairs of a woman during an air raid in WW2. For propaganda purposes the newspapers reported that the deaths arose from a direct hit by a German bomb. Coincidentally, in 2007 an unexploded bomb was uncovered in the area during building work.

In a previous trip to London I had visited the Victoria and Albert Museum in Knightsbridge (next to the Natural History Museum and the Science Museum). The V and A was a great counterpoint to the science based artefacts of its near neighbours. It was opened in 1852 as a Museum of Manufactures, celebrating the art and design aspects rather than the industrial "heavy metal" ones. Just around the corner from Bethnal Green tube station was the V and A Museum of Childhood. I thought that I would pop in for a few minutes to get a flavour of what was on show. I ended up spending a couple of hours in there. It was truly wonderful.

The construction toys section was a kid's delight, and I am a big kid at heart. There was the original Mr Potato Head and all his accessories. When I was young and got a Mr Potato Head the box contained plastic ears, eyes, nose etc. but you had to provide the real potato. Each of these accessories had points to stick into the vegetable. Eventually, safety issues meant that because of the sharp points the toys were banned. Modern sets have a plastic potato – not quite the same magic. Having said that, I love the Mr and Mrs Potato Head characters in the Toy Story films. Talking of potatoes, I once had something called a spud gun. You used to press the end of the barrel into a potato and a piece stuck in it. When you cocked the gun and then pressed the trigger compressed air shot the piece of potato out at quite a speed. Health and Safety? Dream on.

During the centuries many guilds have been set up to oversee the making and quality control of various products; lots of towns have guildhalls. In 1919 Hornby founded the Meccano Guild to link together the many Meccano clubs around the world. I love Meccano. My dear elder brother John, who tragically died in an accident, was given a set for Christmas. That was the only gift given to someone else that I was envious of. John did let me have a go but my efforts at construction were never as grand as his. I am forever thankful that shortly before his death, John and I spent a week together in Torquay (he was twenty one and I was eighteen). The official and emotional end of my childhood occurred shortly after.

***

Christmas was special in a family with six children (yes, my parents were good Catholics). It started with opening the paper streamers and draping them across the living room and pinning them to the ceiling. Balloons were blown up (and frequently burst) before they were tied together with string and then hung from the ceiling too. There would always be a couple left for the kids to play with. We used to hit them through the loops that the streamers had made, occasionally bringing down the decorations. Somehow Dad and Mum were able to keep our presents hidden until Christmas morning despite John and me going on regular search parties. Late one November a large tricycle appeared in the hall and remained there for weeks. Dad said that he was storing it for a neighbour. What joy to see my sister Joy's face when she got it as a present. Dad had managed to fool us all.

I remember one year going to the Christmas party for policemen's children and being given an orange as a present. Well, rationing had not long come to a halt and bringing food in from far flung lands was still a hit and miss affair. Despite that, our Christmas dinners were always banquets with the crunchiest roast potatoes and Mum's sublime sausage meat and chestnut stuffing. I seem to remember that as well as the turkey and all the trimmings there was a vat of curry on the stove for those who fancied something less traditional. Then again, perhaps curry at Christmas was traditional for my parents in India.

All these years later, I still get a buzz when on 1st December I get my bag of Christmas decorations out. Enthusiastically, I put up the tree and adorn it with assorted baubles that have been accumulated over the years; many made when Claire was in primary school. When I was about six I went on a day trip to Southport with my school and bought Mum a plastic nativity scene. It was about two inches square and probably cost a handful of pennies. A few years later she gave it to me. It goes on my tree every year and is called the family heirloom despite being sixty years old and worth less than 10 pence. I even keep it in bubble wrap for goodness sake. On 6th January, with less enthusiasm, I pack the tree, baubles and memories away for another year.

Looking back over the years, giving Mum a plastic toy seems small return for the wonderful life that she has enabled me to lead. Throughout my sixty plus years she has been a loving presence, guiding me effortlessly forward. Bringing up six needy children and being a supportive wife with just a relatively low income could not have been easy. However, never once did I feel neglected or unloved. Parenting is a skill and my Mum should have a PhD in it. Each year, when I put up that plastic nativity, I remember how lucky I have been to have had a mother like her.

***

Back in the museum, there was lots of Meccano on display. Other construction kits were on show too including Lego (and the baby version Duplo), K'nex and Minibrix. I had not heard of the latter. It looked like an early version of Lego to me. Minibrix as a company failed primarily because their product was made from rubber and not plastic. The rubber smelled and shrank as it aged, not a good idea when constructing precision models.

There was as section on children's clothes, from babies to teens. These included boys' dresses. Apparently up to 1920, boys used to wear dresses until they were at least four and sometimes as old as eight. So, Robbie Williams and David Beckham thought that they were fashion icons when they were just copy cats. I am a big fan of Clarks shoes (other brands are available) and was pleased to see a display of their children's shoes. What I learnt was that the company started as early as 1825 and that well into the Victorian age left and right shoes were made in the same identical shape. The museum also had sections on toys, games, dolls and many more. There was a huge display of dolls houses as well as individual houses with quite intricate detail. I would imagine that some of these were definitely to be seen and not played with when originally bought.

Winding my way through the museum I lingered in the section dedicated to the work of Michael Morpurgo, author of the wonderful book and play Warhorse. There was a life size mock-up of the horse. Just past this exhibit I came across what looked like Robby the Robot from the film Forbidden Planet. I have read on numerous occasions that Forbidden Planet is based on Shakespeare's play The Tempest. I'm sorry, but I do not buy that. The alleged links are so tenuous that one could say that the Bette Midler film Hocus Pocus is based on Macbeth because there are three witches in each of them.

The general theme of toys and games in the museum seemed to be that a child has to use their imagination to get the most out of them; play, stimulate, learn. It is a sad indictment of modern society when "If it isn't electrical it isn't any good" seems to be how many older children view toys.

I dragged myself away from the V and A, and made my way along Old Ford Road and used Greenway to cross the River Lea at Iceland Wharf. Avoiding nipping over to see the old Olympic stadium (built for the 2012 London Olympics), now the home of West Ham United football club, I arrived at Stratford. This was to be my first overnight stop and as I was still well within the London sprawl it was yet another cheapish and cheerless (C and C) one. I have mentioned the term cheapish on a number of occasions when describing my stays in London hotels during my road trip. For London, anything under £60 a night for bed and breakfast is relatively cheap unless you want to have no breakfast, share a room or sleep in a bunk house. I am at the age where the phrase bunk house conjures up thoughts of the Roman legions and eight men to a tent. As my next stop would be Romford I hoped this was the last of the C and C hotels I would need to stay at.

Stratford has had a chequered history, moving from agricultural community, to industrial centre, to supporting the docks nearby, to de-industrialisation and decay, to regeneration associated with the London 2012 Olympics, to business and retail parks. Its future seems secure (in the medium term at least) as a modern business centre second only to Canary Wharf. Much was made of the legacy of the 2012 Olympics. Commentators and pundits spent a lot of time discussing this legacy in terms of sporting development. They got it wrong. Britain achieved two more medals in 2016 compared to 2012 and that was with the benefit of Russian athletes being banned. The true legacy of the Olympics is the business regeneration of the area.

Stratford International Railway Station was built at the eastern end of the London Olympic Park. Despite what the name suggests, it is not equipped to handle rail traffic to and from the Continent. It was planned as a stopping point on the high speed rail link but it became unnecessary when someone pointed out the obvious, "why stop here when we are seven minutes from the terminus at

St Pancras?" To save any further embarrassment the International part of the station sign should be quietly removed in the middle of a dark night and placed outside the house of the person who authorised it being built.

Stratford looked like much of modern London (all glass and concrete), so in the morning I quickly made my way to the line of the old Roman road (the A118) and continued my journey northeast.

The next stage of my ramble, from Stratford to Romford, reminded me of the section between Dartford and Blackheath (see chapter 4) where I said "For all but a tiny section I passed only shops and houses with little or no greenery." It was as if the Thames was acting as a giant mirror. Look on Google maps and you will see what I mean. Less than a mile from my start I came through Forest Gate, getting its name from a gate that stopped cattle from straying onto the Roman road. This area would have been part of the great Epping Forest, sadly now much reduced in size and sandwiched between the rivers Lea to the west and Roding to the east. This was the place where only kings and queens could hunt but commoners were allowed to graze their livestock. It is also the setting for a Genesis song, "The Battle of Epping Forest", which tells the story of an east end gang battle. One of the protagonists was the Bethnal Green Butcher and another was Liquid Len and his gang, the Smash Bottle Men. In deference to its history and the song, I popped into the southern-most part of the forest, Wanstead Flats. To get there I had to walk up Dames Road. I thought, how broad minded of the council to dedicate a road to pantomime dames. Sadly, this is not why it was named. Apparently Dame Anna Neagle, star of stage and screen, was born in the area. Another classical (sic) actor who lived there before he achieved worldwide fame was Arnold Schwarzenegger. Another reason for spending some time wandering through Wanstead Flats was because I thought that this would be my only chance to walk on grass until I reached Mountnessing which was still another fifteen miles ahead of me.

On passing under the North Circular Road I reached Ilford and the Roman road went straight as a die through the town centre, and so did I. I quickly ticked off Seven Kings (nothing to do with kings but comes from Sevekyngg meaning settlement of the followers of Seofoca), Goodmayes and Chadwell Heath (claim to fame – it was the terminus of the tram and trolley bus networks from Aldgate). I had no desire to spend any time on this section of my walk as I had seen it all before when I walked from Dartford to Blackheath. And so I ended up at Romford quite early in the afternoon. I had some time to kill as this was my next overnight stop so wandered down a mile or so to the south of the town using the river Rom as my guide. The riverside is home to kingfishers and, would you believe it, green parakeets. Sadly, I saw neither of these species.

Without realising it, I had walked to within three miles of the Thames. In the 19th century a canal company tried, but failed, to build a canal from Romford to the Thames to carry agricultural and industrial produce. At around the same period up to thirty coaches a day called at Romford on their way to and from the capital. I assume the Eastern Counties railway from London which opened in 1839 was the death knell for the coaching business and reduced the need for a canal to take produce to London. On the basis that Romford was outside the cheapish and cheerless hotel range of London I booked with confidence into the Harefield Manor Hotel. Good choice? Yes, very pleasant and close to the start of the next day's walk.

**

In the morning, within half an hour of leaving my hotel I received an email asking me to rate my stay; nothing unusual, as this has happened with most of the hotels I have stayed at in recent years.

One takes this sort of thing for granted as we live in a world of instant global communication. As I walked along the road I mused over this. When my parents emigrated from India in 1947 (separate ships as they were not yet married), the boats took three weeks to make the journey from Bombay (later renamed Mumbai) to Liverpool. Throughout the journeys the boats could communicate almost immediately with India and England. The 19th century was the period when worldwide communication became a possibility between organisations (rather than one to one use by the general public). With the introduction of the telephone, contacting others around the globe became something that the general public could do. However, it took until the late 20th century for individuals to be able to get in touch with numerous others around the world all at the same time, both verbally and visually.

So, how did the Romans manage to communicate through the vast distances of its Empire? The main language of the Romans was Latin. Conquered people slowly learnt the language of their overlords rather than being forced to speak it. Had the Romans remained in Britain and northern Europe the probability is that Latin would have become the standard language. I suppose a modern day role model for coping with different languages in an empire would be the British Empire. For most of the Commonwealth countries, English is the language used for communication between nations. With the expansion of the Empire, English became the world language, and remained so as the Empire shrank.

Then we get to the distances involved and how did the Romans bridge the gaps. Bamber Gascoigne's Historyworld website gives an interesting overview of steps in communication. I love his opening comments regarding shouting messages.

"In modern times 'town criers' hold an annual contest to discover which of them can shout a comprehensible message over the greatest distance. The world record is less than 100 metres. Already, at that short range, a more practical alternative is to run with the message."

Better than running is the use of horses and riders. Gascoigne describes the Persian Empire's method,

"Darius extends the network of roads across the Persian Empire, to enable both troops and information to move with startling speed. At the centre of the system is the royal road from Susa to Sardis, a distance of some 2000 miles (3200 km). At intervals of a day's ride there are posting stations, where new men and fresh horses will be available at any moment to carry a document on through the next day's journey. By this method a message can travel the full distance of the road in ten days, at a speed of about 200 miles a day. A similar road goes down through Syria to the Mediterranean coast and Egypt. Another goes east to India."

He comments on the Romans too,

"The network of Roman roads makes communication steady and reliable, but it is unlikely that it is faster than the delivery system perfected by the Persians - on the terrain of steppe and plateau, across which horsemen can gallop with fine abandon."

In Roman times, the posting stations were called mansiones (between 20 and 35 miles apart) and mutationes (intermediate points). At these places official travellers were able to get fresh horses and even overnight accommodation if required. If there were no facilities available then travellers on Roman business could demand their requirements within prescribed limits.

However, these limits were occasionally ignored by unscrupulous travellers.

By the way, in Latin mille means 1,000. A Roman mille was 1,000 paces, hence the English word mile. A Roman mile is the equivalent of 0.92 miles.

The Romans would have also used the method of lighting beacons to send warnings or a prearranged signal but these were, at best, blunt instruments incapable of communicating complex messages. Crossing the English Channel would have been an ad hoc and relatively unreliable service in Roman times. In later years the cross-channel process became more formal. Gascoigne says,

> *"In 1633 Charles I commissions Thomas Witherings to improve postal communications between England and France. Witherings does so by placing boatmen under contract to make regular crossings with the mail between Dover and Calais. Two years later Charles decides to make the inland mail a royal monopoly, and again selects Witherings for the task."*

For the sake of simplicity let us assume that the Romans could communicate along their road system at a rate of 200 miles per day. London is almost 1,200 miles from Rome so a relay of riders and horses could get between the two cities in six days (plus the time to cross the English Channel). A car could do the same distance in around 20 hours.

***

Back to my walk. I carried on along the route of the Roman road to Gidea Park and then Gallows Corner. True to its name, this was where criminals in the 16th and 17th centuries met their end. At Gallows Corner I had to take a detour as the Roman road became the extremely busy A12. I went via Harold Wood. This was named after the Harold Godwinson who was defeated at the battle of

Hastings. We are a long way from Hastings, I hear you say. Apparently surrounding lands were part of the Godwinson estates. Using Nags Head Lane I passed under the M25 and got back onto the less busy A1023, following the line of the Roman road all the way to Chelmsford. And all the way to Chelmsford and then to Colchester I was able to hear the traffic noise coming from the A12.

The road took me through the centre of Brentwood, and blow me down, what did I find next to the tourist information office? The ruins of a 12th century chapel dedicated to our old friend Thomas Becket. Apparently the ruins were a popular stopping place for pilgrims on their way to Canterbury via a crossing of the Thames near Dartford. It was in Brentwood too that the early rumblings of the Peasants' Revolt started when some people were arrested for non-payment of the poll tax. On the outskirts of Brentwood I came across Larkin's Horse Trough dated 1910. I am not an expert on these things but it was a very nice trough, nestling between a pair of large trees on the well-presented tree-lined High Street. The trough would have come as a welcome stop for the thirsty horses pulling the coaches along this main highway to London. I was feeling thirsty so stopped for a drink and a meal at an old coaching inn and then had an early night at the Brentwood guest house.

Within a blink of an eye after leaving Brentwood I came to Shenfield. Another blink and I was through it and I had open countryside all around me. I was on a lane called Roman Road. For the next seven miles I did a sort of barn dance with the A12. As I walked through Mountnessing, Heybridge, Ingatestone and Margaretting, the A12 bypass went from the left of me then to the right and back to the left. It reminded me of splitting the willow, a dance that involves trying to tie yourself in knots whilst moving in and out of a line of people. When I lived in Worcestershire, my family came to visit and we spent an evening in the village hall dancing to Hetty Peglar's Tump (great name for a band). As none of us had done this sort of dancing before we listened intently to the caller's directions but still got it hopelessly wrong. Then again, most of the others on the floor got it wrong to a greater or lesser degree, much to the annoyance of a pair we christened Fred and Ginger. They had come to dance, not enjoy themselves, and boy, did they take it seriously. At the interval there was the obligatory raffle. One of the prizes was a brace of pheasants. We agreed that for logistical reasons we would not want to win these and would gracefully hand them back if one of us had the winning ticket; they still had their heads, feet and feathers on for goodness sake. I'm not sure what Chris, my brother in law, said during their four hour journey back home, as my sister Lesley proudly put the pheasants in the boot of their new car the following morning.

On the village green in Mountnessing there was a lovely old windmill. For a tiny hamlet it is not short of pubs; I counted three, which is approximately one for every twenty houses by my reckoning. In Ingatestone I counted two pubs and had a late lunch in one of them, the 14th century Star Inn. Apparently there was another pub in this place, the Crown, which was closed by the police. After hours drinking? Short measures? No, for growing cannabis. I was in pub spotting mood, so when I got to Margaretting I counted two (the third having burnt down). So in the space of four sleepy miles there were seven pubs (plus two which had shut down). Now that is what I call a great pub crawl location. Just past Margaretting the A12 made one final swing to the right and I carried straight on, resisting the temptation to do a do-si-do whilst yelling yee-haa. I moseyed on down to the old bunk house in Chelmsford and got a plate of grits and beans at the chuck wagon. Well, I actually booked into a hotel and had an Italian meal in a restaurant.

***

With regards to Chelmsford, Margary (page 247) says,

> *"This was a settlement, Caesaromagus, of some importance as a half-way point to the primary centre, Colchester, and from it an important main road diverged to the north, serving all the western part of East Anglia, where it is known as Peddars Way, and leading eventually to the coast at the mouth of the Wash, perhaps with a ferry to Lincolnshire".*

It was also a settlement of some importance for me too. This was the place where I got my grounding for my career in logistics. However, despite having spent three years of my working life in Chelmsford I didn't recognise the place, none of it. Surely things could not have changed that much in thirty five years? Then it came back to me, the three years were a fog that time and booze had thickened to a smog. In those days I lodged with one of my work colleagues, Jack, a bronzed Adonis of Italian parentage who was a magnet for females. However, as a true friend Jack was happy propping up the bar with his mates whilst fending off gorgeous looking women. Eventually he met a lovely lady and settled down. He had two children, Dominic and Victoria, who I am convinced to this day were named after local off-licences that we frequented, Peter Dominic and Victoria Wine. The assistant manager, another of my drinking pals, was a man of principles. During Lent he observed the Catholic tradition of abstinence and each year for forty days he went through the period by refusing to drink tonic in his gin. What will power. My depot manager was a legend in his own lunch time. He had the run of Chequers, a local inn where he would hold regular meetings with his managers and shop stewards. One evening after a session in the pub, I walked a lady back to her house and was invited in for a cup of coffee. I thought that she was obviously from a well to do family judging from the size of the palatial accommodation. The next day Jack informed me that I had been to the nurses' home.

After a night in the hotel, there were three places that I wanted to visit in Chelmsford; the depot that I worked at, the Chequers inn and also the large park that I seemed to remember being somewhere close to my place of work. During my shifts I used to pop out to Hylands Park and spend my dinner breaks relaxing in the serenity. The place inspired me to write some brilliant poetry there. When I recently dug out the folder containing this verse (for the first time in thirty years) I can confirm that it is truly ... awful. Even the great McGonnagall would have been embarrassed by it. Thankfully, the park is still there in all its tranquillity and my folder is locked away again. Unknowingly, I had walked right past the park the previous evening on my way in to Chelmsford. I then walked from the park to Widford Road, site of the old industrial estate. It was obvious that the depot had long since been demolished and some rather plush houses erected in its place. Even the first factory and associated industries built by radio communications pioneer Marconi are long gone. Being just over half an hour on the train from London, Chelmsford is a prime commuter location in addition to being the county town of Essex. Next stop was Chequers for a spot of lunch of the non-liquid variety. Whilst there, I enquired whether anybody remembered the depot manager and his entourage. Sadly, we weren't even a distant memory.

Forlornly, I wandered back into town. Sorry, I should say city. Chelmsford has the honour of being the last town in England to have been granted city status in 2012. Nothing stirred in the recesses of my mind so when I stumbled upon Central park with an impressive Victorian railway viaduct (see below) and the beautiful Norman cathedral my hankering for the past disappeared. It is a waste of time to dwell on the past that cannot be changed when there is much to see in the present and look forward to in the future. If one phrase could sum up my philosophy of life it is "Don't dwell on the past, live in the present and plan for the future".

Chelmsford has a racecourse too. Now, I certainly don't remember there being one when I lived there. I am not really a high rolling betting man (I limit my stake to ten pounds when visiting a track) but I do like the atmosphere of a live race meeting. Surely I would have gone at least once in my three years there. What I do remember as if it were yesterday is going on a day out with staff from work at Chelmsford all the way to Epsom, with its fairground in the centre of the course. The year that I went Shergar won the Derby by miles. If you have never been to a race meeting I recommend Cartmel at the southern edge of the Lake District. It is in a quite beautiful setting and also has a fun fair set up in the centre of the racecourse. So, how come I didn't remember Chelmsford's racecourse? For the simple reason that it did not exist when I lived there. The racecourse opened in 2008, went into receivership nine months later and then reopened in 2015. It is an all-weather track but there are plans afoot to lay a turf track alongside it.

Whilst on the subject of betting, when in Las Vegas (stopover for one night whilst on a walking holiday) I limited myself to ten dollars ante when I visited Caesar's Palace casino. Much to my surprise I almost doubled my stake to eighteen dollars. I was more interested in seeing the other punters. What shocked me was the robotic way people fed the fruit machines. Winning was not the driving force here, it was all to do with feeding these insatiable light and sound monsters, the modern equivalent of the old one armed bandits. When I was a child Dad used to take us to the fair in Wythenshawe Park and we always had a go on these rusty old machines, one old penny per go (240 pennies per pound). It used to take all my strength just to pull the lever. I would then eagerly watch the three lines of fruit rolling around. We never came away with any winnings. If you were lucky enough to get anything out of these rigged machines you fed it straight back in.

Despite being very busy, I found Chelmsford a cheerless and uninviting place. The pedestrianised shopping area with its people moving in all directions did little to alleviate my isolation. Many buildings will have sprung up since my last visit to the place and all of them seem to have been built with one eye on the prize for the worst eyesore in the city. Even the park from where I took my photograph of the viaduct was soulless and uninviting.

I gladly waved farewell to Chelmsford and, following closely to the line of the old Roman road, using Springfield road and Main road, I headed towards Colchester. After only a few minutes I took a detour north to look at New Hall School. This independent Catholic school, catering for boarders and day students, is based around a building which formed part of one of Henry VIII's estates. I went to a Catholic school that catered for boarders and day students and wanted to do a comparison. Okay, I appreciate that the Essex countryside is not a built up area of Manchester but blimey, what a place. Both the building (an ex palace) and the setting were wonderful. The only green near my school was Alexandra Park. I used to love walking through it on the way to school, feeding the ducks on the pond with my Marmite on toast (sorry Mum). I love Marmite, especially on almost cremated toast. Even now, Mum, who is well into her nineties, will make a batch of Marmite on toast "for the journey".

Whilst on the subject of food, it is amazing how certain smells can instantly take you back in time. Every time I open a bag of smoky bacon crisps I am transported back to my days at school. Our playing fields were about two miles walk from the school. On Wednesday afternoons students quickly made their way to the rugby/football fields and got ready in the old changing room, with its wooden floors and unique odour. No, the smell wasn't smoky bacon crisps, I am coming to that. I enjoyed my games of rugby but less so the showers. Do plumbers design all school showers in the same way, either scalding hot or cold enough to freeze the proverbials off a brass monkey? It was worth the torture though as I always popped in to the tuck shop that was part of the changing room complex and, you guessed, had a bag of smoky bacon crisps.

Back to New Hall. Okay it wins in terms of location and building, but does it have as good a motto as my old school? "The Best Start in Life" versus "In Novitate Vitae (towards new life)". Huh, they don't even have their motto in Latin. Then again both mottos fall a long way short of "Learn or Leave" I mentioned earlier in the book. Come to think about it, my old school seems to have changed its motto. When I was there I am sure it was something like "Nunquam oteo torpebat" which I think means "never torpedo your otter". Having said that, I only just squeezed a pass in my Latin O level.

It is said that schooldays are the best days of your life. I can honestly say that my seven years at St Bede's were truly wonderful. I was only ever bullied the one time, not by a teacher but a pupil. Once my Mum had sorted out both him and his mum he and I became mates. As to teachers and bullying, those were less enlightened days. When we witnessed the new PE master, fresh from the tougher version of the SAS, making poor, rotund, non-athlete Stanley hang from the wall bars for the whole lesson all the others were thinking the same, "Thank goodness he's not picking on me". Another rather round pupil, Bubbles (yes we kids can be so thoughtful when doling out nicknames) was well liked by the PE teacher because he was a good hooker at rugby. My best pal at school, Flossy, introduced me to the Air Training Corps and my first flight in an aeroplane. You used to have to wear a parachute in an RAF Chipmunk and, by crikey, were the straps tight in all the wrong places. On leaving school, Flossy became an airline pilot. Sadly he was killed over what was then Yugoslavia in a mid-air collision.

Retracing my steps from New Hall I then carried on through Boreham and Hatfield Peverel and reached Witham. Boreham had a quaint church, but what really caught my eye was the Old Rectory opposite. It was a huge white and black Tudor style building that seemed far larger than the church. In each of these three places I kept stumbling upon very old buildings. Witham had one with a date of 1300. Whereas Boreham and Hatfield Peverel could still be classed as large villages, Witham has definitely outgrown that description. It also has the dubious honour of being the site of the worst rail crash in Essex with regards to loss of life. In 1905 the London outbound express to Cromer was speeding through the station when it derailed. Eleven people (including one who was on the platform) died and over seventy were seriously injured. Opposite the library there is the equivalent of a London blue plaque (which provide details of famous people who lived in the buildings where the plaques are stuck to). There is a statue of crime writer Dorothy L. Sayers, author of the Lord Peter Wimsey series. She lived in Witham and I stopped overnight at the White Hart hotel.

In the morning I had a potential problem. The route ahead should have me walking partway along the A12. This would have been a serious health risk so I got a bus to Kelvedon, stopped for a while, and then another bus from Kelvedon to Marks Tey. Whilst in Kelvedon, just for something to do, I popped into the Norman church, St Mary the Virgin, a grade 1 listed building. Before the A12 bypass was built it must have been a living hell in Witham and Kelvedon, coping with the huge volume of traffic. The same could be said for those sleepy villages west of Chelmsford that I had passed through previously. A short bus ride got me to Marks Tey. When I worked in Chelmsford we used to deliver to Marks Tey and I always had it in my mind that it was a huge place close to the sea (subliminal link to the Tay Bridge perhaps?). It is tiny and nowhere near the sea. Having got off the bus the only huge things I saw were the roundabout system, the A12 and the railway line. I had no option but to walk down to the Red Lion for a very early lunch.

As it would only take me just over an hour to reach Colchester I decided on a slight detour north of the town, passing through Eight Ash Green and Fordham Heath, and ended up in West Bergholt (previously called Bergholt Sackville). Now this small village really does punch above its weight with regards to religious matters. A Bronze Age cemetery containing ten graves was found just south of the village. Pottery dates it to around 1000BC. Moving on swiftly a couple of millennia and Queen Elizabeth I was informed on two occasions of wrongdoings in the village. On the first she was notified that a vicar was spending too much time in the inns and not enough tending his flock. On the second a vicar refused to conduct the service in English, wishing to do it in Latin, and he also said that the Queen's reforms were politically incorrect. Despite this obvious treason he escaped punishment but eventually was removed from office by Elizabeth. During the Civil War a vicar was accused of drunkenness and swearing whilst conducting services and also preaching royalist sermons. No punishment is recorded against him. These three less than virtuous role models of the parish seem to have got off lightly for their breaches. Not so Agnes George. She became one of the Stratford Martyrs (eleven men and two women) who were tried and burnt at the stake at Stratford, London in 1556 for their Protestant views during the reign of Queen Mary. Agnes' first "crime" was refusing to attend church services that were conducted in the Catholic tradition. Then, whilst in Newgate prison, she accused the Pope of being the Anti-Christ. Twenty thousand people attended her burning. The Stratford Martyrs memorial, in St John's, Stratford Broadway, commemorates the likes of Agnes George and others persecuted during the reign of Bloody Mary. I had walked right past that only recently and yet had not noticed it.

Following my detour I headed warily into Colchester, expecting a repeat of the ugly sprawl of Chelmsford city centre. As you will see in the next chapter, was I in for a surprise?

7 COLCHESTER (CAMULODUNUM)

Colchester obviously had a history long before it became the first Roman town in Britain. Tools and pottery dating from the Stone, Bronze and Iron Ages have been found in the area. However, the archaeological record is far from complete. Sometimes it is just pot luck to find a pot that can be identified from a specific time and place. What can be said with a greater degree of certainty is that the distribution of Celtic place names gives a good clue as to the extent of the Celtic language, not least in Essex. By 2000BC it was one of the main languages in mainland Europe and the British Isles.

It is believed that the heads of the Catuvellauni (including Cunobelin, father of Caratacus) could have been client kings of Rome. When a territory was conquered the Romans sometimes set up a client king to run the area on their behalf, thus ensuring alliance and allegiance to Rome. In places where there had been no conquest, client kings may also have been agreed. This produced a relatively secure frontier for both Romans and non-Romans alike. Another benefit was that two-way trade and wealth generation would be easier under these circumstances. Excavation of late Iron Age burial sites at Colchester support the notion that the Catuvellauni kings had such an arrangement (at least those before Caratacus became leader). Items dated around 15BC at a site at Lexden in Colchester suggest a pro Roman person of high status was buried there.

So, just prior to the Roman invasion, Celtic Colchester was a major focal point for movement of people and goods. Easy access to the

North Sea via the river Colne meant that import and export were relatively easy. According to Patricia Southern in "Roman Britain a New History 55BC-AD450" (page 52),

> *"The finds at the Sheepen site* [centre of the settlement] *showed that the Catuvellauni developed an almost insatiable desire for Roman goods. Amphora carrying oil and wine are abundant, and good Roman pottery and metalwork are found in quantity, possibly arriving with shiploads of more perishable luxuries which have not survived."*

No doubt along with the influx of Roman goods, tales of the might of the Empire would have permeated British society. Whereas the Romans could be generous to defeated opponents, they could also take bloody revenge. Loss of liberty (sold into slavery) and seizure of property were threats that potential foes were well aware of. So, the Catuvellauni were not ignorant of the strength of the Romans nor of what they did to people who opposed them.

Due to overwhelming strength of numbers, and perhaps because they remembered the crushing defeat at the Medway and knew of the reputation of the Romans, Claudius' army brushed aside Caratacus and his Catuvellauni warriors. Camulodunum was captured and the first Roman capital set up there. The Catuvellauni were disarmed. The message to other tribes was clear, "Work with us or suffer the consequences." The defeat had the desired effect, with up to eleven tribes surrendering prior to Claudius' return to Rome. The rest of his army was left behind to carry out the dirty work of consolidation and expansion.

David Mattingly, in "An Imperial Possession, Britain in the Roman Empire", gives a chronological list of the main campaigns and battles from AD43-83 (pages 97-98). In those forty years he lists fourteen major campaigns. Consolidation in the southeast would seem easy compared to expansion. However, apart from the Iceni revolt of AD60-61, the southeast did remain relatively pacified and supply lines to and from the continent secure. I will not linger further on the fine detail of the expansion programme for the simple reason that there is no fine detail. Patricia Southern (page 80) says,

> "The ensuing campaigns in Britain while Plautius was still in command cannot be constructed in detail. The whereabouts of the legions can be suggested by extrapolating backwards from the points where they created their first, more permanent legionary fortresses, and sometimes it is possible to suggest their intermediate stopping points from the remains of camps, but the overall picture is considered to be much more fluid and complicated than the archaeology is able to illustrate."

Caratacus escaped to modern day Wales, but not to retire just yet. He joined the Silures tribe and fought an indecisive battle in south Wales, then moved to north Wales and with the Ordovices tribe fought again. Eventually, defeated but not yet ready to throw in the towel, Caratacus fled to northern England to Cartimandua, queen of the Brigantes. Unfortunately for him, she had a client ruler relationship with the Romans so he was handed over to them.

On being sent to Rome as a prisoner of war, Caratacus impressed Claudius with his demeanour and was allowed to retire peacefully in Italy with his family. Now he is a person who led a busy life. I'm surprised that Mel Gibson did not make a film about him, with Gibson obviously in the starring role. Then again, Caratacus did not come to a grisly end like William Wallace whom Gibson portrayed on screen. Perhaps he could have depicted Vercingetorix, the Gallic warrior who was taken to Rome by Julius Caesar, imprisoned for six years and finally executed.

And Claudius? He had been absent from Rome for six months, of which only sixteen days were spent in Britain. Once back home, he celebrated a grand triumph, receiving the title Britannicus. Unlike Caratacus, he did not spend his final years in quiet retirement. Claudius had become a reluctant emperor on the death of Caligula in AD41 and within two years had overseen the start of the Roman invasion of Britain. His first marriage to Messalina ended when she and Silius, her lover, were killed following a conspiracy against Claudius. Ever unlucky in love, Claudius then married his niece, Agrippina, mother of future emperor Nero, and was poisoned by her in AD54.

Aulus Plautius, the commander of the invasion force probably fared somewhat better than his boss, Claudius. In four years under his leadership, the Romans advanced to the course of what became known as Fosse Way, roughly territory south of a line between the rivers Severn and Humber. He left Britain in AD47 and arrived in Rome in triumph. We do not know for certain what eventually became of him. If you believe the film Quo Vadis (1951) he became a Christian and was crucified and burned to death in the Colosseum. Then again the Aulus Plautius in the film could have been the son of the conquering hero. In short, we do not know for certain what happened to Plautius after he was welcomed back in Rome as a hero.

What we do know with a fair degree of certainty is that whilst the other legions carried on the advance further inland, the XX Legion based itself in Colchester which very rapidly became the first centre of the Roman occupation. Lindsay Allason-Jones in "Women in Roman Britain" (page 67-68) says,

> *"The Roman was an essentially urban being: political activities, social life and commerce all revolved around the town. Iron Age Britain, by comparison, was agricultural and the majority of people lived in small groups … As her*

Empire expanded Rome made the establishment of towns a priority, not only because towns were seen to be a vital factor in civilising primitive people, but also because they simplified the administration of a new province. "

Camulodunum, one of the model towns known as coloniae, was founded in AD49, and would have been populated initially by legionary veterans. Allason-Jones goes on to say (page 68),

"The inhabitants of coloniae would have been regarded as the elite. The majority were full Roman citizens, although many of their wives would have been provincials, and a number of non-citizens, known as incolae, would also have been residents."

As the town grew, so did the amenities, including baths, forum, theatre and temples. Even traces of a circus (for chariots, not clowns) have been found within the city. For security a stone wall, the oldest in Britain, was built, but not until after the Boudiccan revolt (closing the stable door after the horse has bolted?). The Britons would have been used to hill forts with their earthworks, banks and ditches. I would imagine that the impact of this wall on the local tribes would have been as threatening as the Norman castles would become to the Anglo-Saxons who had taken the Roman wall model as their template. Another knock on effect of the revolt was that the provincial capital moved to Londinium. However, Camulodunum remained a major town throughout the Roman occupation of Britain.

The large Roman temple (one of at least seven) appeared in the centre. There was a mock-up of it in the museum. This temple was a constant and stark reminder to the Catuvellauni of their conquest and subjugation. Also, the Britons had their first experience of the Imperial Cult with its building. The worship and glorification of a dead Roman would help maintain ties with the centre of the Empire for those a long way from home.

It is interesting to note that worship of local gods was not usually frowned on if it did not impinge upon Roman security.

The castle (see below) was eventually built on the site of where the temple originally stood. Patricia Southern says (page 82),

> "... and its [the temple] *podium is preserved as the foundation for William the Conqueror's equally massive castle.*"

Once the headquarters were set up at Colchester, the day to day administration had to be undertaken. For new towns that the Romans created, other than Colchester, a model similar to our current one (Prime Minister in 10 Downing Street and Chancellor of the Exchequer next door at number 11) was used. The Romans had the governor looking at law and order, transport, communication and security, and a procurator looking after the finance (whilst reporting to the governor).

Teams of civil servants would have supported both governor and procurator. As the invasion expanded then the governor would have set up chains of command for each new town. Due to the limited speed of communication these towns were semi-autonomous and those in charge would have control over the surrounding territory. As is ever the case, some of these towns would be run by fair and responsible bureaucrats whereas others had corrupt officials in charge. Client kings will have also played an important part in the governance of towns under their control.

Colchester was an exception to the model town as this was the first one set up in a hostile and as yet unconquered Britain. The town was placed under full military supervision. A legionary fortress and fort were built. It was not until AD49 and the movement of XX Legion out to support the military advances that a veterans' colony was established. Only then was the urban model able to be established in terms of administration and local government.

When I first arrived on the outskirts of Colchester, before moving southeast along the Roman road line into the city, I noticed a road called Cymbeline Way. Shakespeare's play, Cymbeline, is supposed to be based on a real king, Cunobelin. Cunobelin, as mentioned earlier, was the father of Caratacus (peaceful retirement in Rome) and Togodumnus (killed after the battle of the Medway) whom we have already come across. He had a third son, Adminius a pro-Roman, who was exiled in AD40 and fled to the then emperor, Caligula. In a similar way to Verica asking for Claudius' help when he was exiled, Adminius tried to get Caligula's support. A planned invasion of Britain never took place and Caligula was soon after assassinated and replaced by Claudius. I keenly read the play to see if I could recognise anything I had uncovered during my road trip research. The only involvement to do with Romans are, firstly there is roman-tic treachery and secondly Cymbeline's two sons help to defeat the Romans (what?). Cymbeline has a third child, a daughter called Imogen, who marries against her father's will. She dresses up as a boy and not even her father or husband recognise her (for goodness sake). Cymbeline's son-in-law is exiled and ends up in Rome like Cunobelin's third son, Adminius. There is an Iago type baddie with a similar name, Iachimo (which means little Iago apparently). The play is set in the time of the Roman emperor Augustus (reigned from 27BC to AD14) when there were no Romans in Britain for Cymbeline and his sons to fight. To me, it looks like Shakespeare has taken the pages and plot lines from other plays, tossed them down the stairs and grabbed those that landed furthest and wrote Cymbeline along with all the anachronisms and historical inaccuracies.

High horse time. Yet again, in Cymbeline, Shakespeare uses the ploy of dressing up one of the female characters as a male. I know that Shakespeare is part of this country's literary heritage but how could the same person write plays of genius (King Lear, Hamlet and Macbeth) as well as some utterly stupid ones involving men being duped by women posing as men. I recently watched a production of As You Like It and could not believe how crass the story was. Okay, I accept that the use of language was excellent but I could not get past the banality of the plot. On the other hand, the film Shakespeare in Love uses the "woman dressing as a man" ploy brilliantly and the Merchant of Venice, one of Shakespeare's masterpieces, does have two women fooling men when they dress up as a lawyer and his male clerk. Whoa Dobbin, time to get off my high horse.

Anyway, back to Colchester. I had intended to spend only a short while there and then go to London for the night. As it turned out I dallied a lot longer than planned and so booked into the George hotel, a medieval coaching inn. One bonus was that I would not have to spend the night in a C and C hotel in London prior to starting my trek up Ermine Street. Sometimes you stumble on things that you were not expecting. In the hotel, whilst walking up to my bedroom, I passed a wall on the stairs that was in need of serious repair, as I first thought. On further inspection (and after reading a plaque) I realised that this was the original wattle and daub that the owners of the hotel had uncovered and left for all to see. Well done, the George hotel.

The hotel is on the High Street, close to the impressive town hall building. What I liked about High Street was that it did not have modern high rise glass and concrete buildings hemming me in. Also, it was not pedestrianised. It was a one-way street with only one lane for buses and cars. This steady flow of traffic seemed to add to the ambience of the town centre. I drifted slowly down to the park and its well-attended play area. It was quite wonderful and proudly standing at the highest point was the castle. I spent a couple of hours inside. Here I learnt about both local Roman and

Anglo Saxon history and saw a couple of original Roman tombstones.

There was also a section dedicated to the English Civil War. It was at the walled town of Colchester that remnants of the Royalist army made a final stand long after Charles 1st had been defeated. Due to strength of numbers, they took over the town which had been loyal to the Parliamentarians during the war. Following a long siege, during which illness and starvation became rife, the Royalists were defeated. Sadly many of the loyal Parliamentarian townsfolk died during and after the siege was lifted.

During my amble around the town I came across extensive remnants of the Roman wall and then arrived at the Balkerne Gate (see both below). This is the largest surviving Roman gateway in Britain and was built not long after the Boudiccan revolt. What particularly pleased me was that it is still used by people in the town as a thoroughfare.

A sign for the Natural History Museum, housed in an old church, drew me to it; very quaint and extremely informative. Here, I learnt about the geological and natural history of the area.

Next, I wandered down to the ruins of St Botolph's Abbey. Even to an untrained eye like mine it was obvious that it had been built out of the same stone as the castle. Both of these buildings had used spoila from the Roman buildings that fell into disrepair and decay once the imperial invaders had left these shores.

The town does not just have ancient history to offer. At the top of High Street I came across two large brass coloured elephants, one pointing the way to the castle and the other to the railway station. On the street down to the railway station every so often I came cross brass plaques on the pavements informing people of various facts and buildings. Then at the railway station I saw another huge brass elephant (see below). Also, not far from the Balkerne Gate is a colossal 19th century water tower called the Jumbo Tower.

So what was it with Colchester's fixation with elephants? Obviously, to me they must be to celebrate the fact that Claudius had brought these giant beasts with him when he led the conquest of the town. Wrong! The Jumbo in question was born in Sudan in 1860, bought by London Zoo and then controversially sold in 1882 to Barnum and Bailey's circus. The great animal died in Ontario in 1885 following a collision with a railway engine. Colchester has its own zoo (rated as 11th best in the world and number 2 in the UK) but time did not permit me to pay it a visit.

Talking of zoos, reminds me of the times I have visited Chester Zoo. I still vividly remember when I was six and got stung by a wasp. Whilst eating an ice cream it landed on the cone, unseen by me. I put my right thumb on the wasp and felt a sharp stinging pain. Ooh, I cried. At the first aid tent iodine was put on the injury. Apart from that I always enjoyed my trips to Chester Zoo, either with my parents and siblings or my ex-wife and Claire. It is a wonderful place. I especially like the bat cave. In here, it is dark, but light enough to see bats, large and small, silently gliding within inches of your face. You can even feel the ripples of air as they pass by. When I lived in Lostock, near Bolton, the tiny bats would come out at dusk. It was wonderful watching them zig zag noiselessly, chasing moths and other flying insects that seemed invisible to the naked eye. The silence of the bats is quite eerie. One half expects a submarine sonar beep or at least a bird like tweet to come from them as they fly.

Before entering Colchester I had been expecting another Chelmsford and not a Canterbury or Rochester which both have history oozing out of their streets. However, at the end of my walk around the town I realised that Colchester can stand proudly alongside its more illustrious Kentish counterparts. It has even endured some recent kicks in the teeth. It had to readjust to not being a garrison town on the scale of previous years. When I lived in Essex, Colchester was home to a major army presence. In the last thirty years the size of the garrison has reduced substantially with much of the land previously owned by the Ministry of Defence having been sold off for housing development. Still based here is the country's only Military Corrective Training Unit. All three armed forces use this facility. It is more commonly known as "The Glasshouse" and is used to hold the naughty service men and women. Also, Colchester lost out to local rival Chelmsford in 2012 when it tried to upgrade from town to city status and the previous year it failed in its bid to be recognised as a world heritage site. Sadly even the zoo was not immune to bad news. Ten year old Telu, a Komodo dragon that sired 24 offspring, died suddenly in November 2017. Telu and his partner, Mutu, were the first dragons in the country to breed by natural methods. Many of his offspring were shipped to other European zoos as part of the European Endangered Species Programme.

Having reached as far as Claudius had, it was now time to retrace my route back to London (using the train rather than by foot). I was now ready to tackle the long slog north up the entire length of Ermine Street to York.

8 LONDON (BISHOPSGATE) TO BRAUGHING

Route: Margary 2a (pages 194-198).

Having conquered the Catuvellauni and entered their capital in triumph, the tasks of the Romans were now two fold, consolidation and expansion. As mentioned previously, Roman expansion did not rely solely on conquest. Their strength also lay in the many alliances with local client kings and tribes. The most famous alliance was with Togidubnus who was based near Chichester on the south coast. He eagerly took on the trappings of the Roman way of life, as evidenced by the remains of his sumptuous palace at Fishbourne. Togidubnus was well rewarded for his loyalty, including being given extra land that was previously held by the Atrebates and Belgae. Ivan Margary lived close to Fishbourne and financed the excavation of the site. Another client king was Prasutagus of the Iceni. In simplistic terms, in the first four years of the Roman invasion the four legions were involved with the following:

Legio II Augusta, commanded by future emperor Vespasian, went south and southwest.

Legio XIV Germina was tasked with the conquest and subjugation of the west and northwest.

Legio XX Valeria Victrix remained around Colchester to maintain control of territory already conquered.

Legio IX Hispana was to move north in the general direction of what would become Ermine Street. It would reach the banks of the Trent and Humber within four years. I would take slightly less time (chapters 8 to 12). By AD61 the Legion had still only got as far as the north bank of the Humber but in the meantime was almost wiped out by Prasutagus's wife, Boudicca (chapter 12). York and all points north (except Cumbria), to what would become Hadrian's Wall, would not be pacified until AD74, almost thirty years after the original invasion by Plautius. And this army and its animals would have needed regular supplies of food, drink and other daily necessities.

During my ambles through Kent, London and Essex I had been able to take both food and drink (water and the occasional beer) almost at will. The modern traveller is spoilt for choice when it comes to the variety of provisions on offer and what time of day or night they can be obtained. So, how did a Roman army of conquest and occupation cope with the logistics of supply? Jonathan Roth's book, "The Logistics of the Roman Army at War (264BC-AD235)" was a fascinating read that answered my question. As mentioned previously in the Preamble, I have had two careers; logistics management and then teaching. Perhaps it was the many years in this first profession that made Roth's book seem so alive. Or maybe I was becoming a Roman nerd without realising it?

Logistics is a fairly modern term. Basically it can be boiled down into the five Rights; get the Right product, to the Right place, at the Right time, in the Right manner, at the Right cost. This is what service is all about and to that extent servicing an army is no different than delivering to someone in their home, albeit on a grander and somewhat riskier scale. Having said that I do remember delivering a small parcel once. When it was no more than halfway through the letter box a vicious sounding dog grabbed the package and tore it to shreds. Counting my fingers, I made my way back to the van wondering if the people in the house ever got the chance to read any mail the postman delivered.

Before reading Roth's book I had no inkling as to the scale of task of ensuring that men and beasts were well supplied. The range of materials a Roman army took with it was huge. Roth (page 2) says,

"The Roman army took a vast array of materials into the field: clothing, armor [the American spelling], edged weapons, missiles, tents, portable fortifications, cooking gear, medical supplies, writing materials, and much more … Yet, approximately ninety percent of the weight of the supplies needed by an ancient army was made up of only three elements: food, fodder and firewood."

Roman armies took two meals a day; breakfast (prandium) in the morning and their main meal (cena) prior to lights out. Sometimes, ahead of a battle, soldiers would have the chance to eat their main meal in case the fight was a long one. The following is taken from Roth's figures (page 43) for the average daily ration of a soldier on active service:

Item	grams	calories	protein (grams)
Grain	850	1,950	75
Or bread	850	ditto	ditto
Or biscuit	650	ditto	ditto
Roasted meat/pork	160	640	15
Vegetables (lentils)	40-50	170	10
Cheese	27	90	0
Olive oil	40	350	10
Wine/vinegar	160	190	0
Salt	40	0	0
Total	1,117-1,327	3,390	142

I could get by with that as long as I were allowed to swap the salt and vinegar for smoky bacon crisps. Roth further says (page 43),

> "In fact, all the evidence indicates that the diet of the Roman soldier was excellent, both in quality and quantity. It is noteworthy among complaints aired by mutinous legionaries in AD14, none concerned bad food, normally a commonplace of military griping."

How the milled grain was prepared depended on circumstances. It was sometimes eaten as a mush or porridge made by adding water, salt and oil. Bread was often made out of the grain. So, who baked it? The legionaries made their bread on open hearths, one hearth per contuberium (tent unit, consisting of eight men). This allowed for flexibility whilst on the road and less reliance on central bakeries which would have required dismantling and erecting each night. There is some evidence that auxiliaries had their food prepared by cooks. When not on a campaign, or if rapid movement precluded the milling of the grain and reduced the availability of firewood, the grain ration was made into biscuits in advance. These biscuits could last for over a month, compared to the bread which had a shelf life of less than a week. Officers ate a better diet than mere squaddies.

Horses (for cavalry use and not as beasts of burden), donkeys, mules and oxen also needed food and water. Food was of three types: hard fodder (grain such as oats and barley), green or dry fodder (various crops grown on farms; hay, straw, clover, vetch), pasturage (food that the animals ate whilst grazing in the fields).

We know what the animals ate from the study of equine coprolites (dried horse manure) found in military camps.

Imagine a careers office in school:

"So, what do you want to do when you grow up?"

"I'd like to study dried horse sh.. er, coprolites miss."

Roth details amounts required per animal (pages 66-67),

(Kilograms)	Hard	or	Dry/Green	or	Pasturage	Water
Donkey	1.5		5.0		10.0	20 lt
Mule	2.0		6.0		12.0	20 lt
Horse	2.5		7.0		14.0	30 lt
Oxen	7.0		11.0		22.0	30 lt

Supplies of fresh water and firewood for cooking and warmth tended to be found close to where camps were set up. In Roman times there would have been a far greater expanse of forests in Britain than we see nowadays.

Now let us consider who transported all of the supplies. Legionaries were trained to carry considerable loads, thus reducing the number of baggage trains. However, the greater the load the slower the march. In addition to his rations a soldier had responsibility for his clothing and weapons, cooking gear and tools. Some debate as to the total weight carried by soldiers has meant that there is no definitive figure. It could have been 25kg plus rations (which depended on days allowed). Seventeen days rations may have weighed 20kg so the total load was 45kg (or just under 100lb in old money). Soldiers would have been expected to carry five days rations as the norm.

Each contuberium (eight men to a tent, remember) would have had a mule that carried the shared equipment; tent and accessories (40kg), mill for grinding (27kg), tools and baskets (18.7kg), cooking pot (0.6kg), pack saddle (20kg) and 16 pila muralia (39.2kg). The latter were long wooden spikes, sharpened at both ends, which were used to safeguard the encampments at night.

Then there were baggage trains that carried a variety of equipment, including the officers' personal effects. Roth comments on these trains (page 81),

> *"The size of the trains that followed an army was an important factor in the ability of the army to move and fight. A lack of carrying capacity reduced the army's combat capability, but too large a train could restrict movement."*

A Roman legion had no non-combatants. All men were expected to fight. Those that drove the mules or baggage trains were exempt from fatigue duty but were still front line soldiers. They were called immunes. Any non-combatants (servants, slaves) were ancillary to a legion and not part of its number.

So, we now know how much the army needed and how it was carried. But where did it get the supplies from? Some foraging off the land did take place, especially for water and wood. It is not clear whether this was undertaken by the soldiers or slaves. Another way of obtaining supplies was by requisition; sending out requests for local inhabitants to bring supplies to a camp. Pillaging, the forceful stealing of supplies and destruction of property, was seen as the least preferred option. This wasn't due to not wanting to upset the indigenous population but more as a matter of maintaining the discipline of the soldiers. Obtaining supplies in the above three ways was crucial, as Roth (page 306) says,

> *"Drawing supplies from the area of operations was always an important part of pre-modern logistics. "Living off the land" was not a haphazard activity; rather, it demanded a great deal of planning and organisation."*

The rest of the needs of an army would have come from its storage bases and the use of supply lines. The bases were of three types; the strategic base from which supplies were drawn, the operational base that covered an area of activity, and the tactical base in the army's immediate vicinity. Roman roads, forts and overnight encampments played an important role in this as did many ports located both at the sea shore and at points on navigable rivers.

Napoleon once said, "An army marches on its stomach". In Roman times too, lack of food, fodder, firewood and water would have rapidly turned an efficient, well managed and motivated fighting force into a ramshackle rabble, incapable of sustained warfare and movement. Safeguarding one's own supplies and disrupting an opponents were essential day to day aspects of an army both on the march and in barracks.

***

I arrived at Liverpool St Station from Colchester, which was very handy as Bishopsgate is just on its doorstep. This was the start of Ermine St. The name is derived from the tribe (Earningas) that was based in the area after the Roman occupation, and, in common with the other Roman roads in Britain, was not named by the Romans. It was called Earninga Straete. I was keen to set off towards York and avoid stopping at a C and C hotel. Using the well-tried maxim of "If it ain't broke, don't fix it" modern road planners have taken the routes of many Roman roads and built up to date major trunk roads. I had already seen this with the A2 in Kent and the A12 in Essex and Ermine Street was no exception. The modern A10 follows closely to the original line of Ermine Street from London to Braughing. I would walk on roads and paths that ran parallel with it when the A10 got too dangerous.

Margary (page 194) says that,

> *"Next to Watling Street this road* [Ermine Street] *was perhaps the most important thoroughfare in Britain, for it*

was designed to give direct communication to the main centres of the military occupation at Lincoln and York."

The route that Watling Street took to the northwest may have been influenced by existing tracks. However, on the route that I was travelling Margary further states (page 194) that,

"With Ermine Street, however, they were very literally breaking new ground, for it is unlikely that a direct northern track upon anything like this line had ever existed."

I started breaking my new ground at Bishopsgate. Coming out of Liverpool Street Station and onto the A10, towards the southeast I spied the top of the building known as the Gherkin. This office block is built on the site of the old Baltic Exchange which was extensively damaged by an IRA bomb in 1992. Conservationists and English Heritage wanted the building to be reconstructed and so careful dismantling of some of the damaged remains took place. Somewhere along the way they were sold and ended up in Estonia in the Baltic, of all places, awaiting incorporation into their commercial area. Proving that some architects have a sense of humour, we ended up with the Gherkin. Unable to get a good view of this building I walked south along Bishopsgate to try to see more of it. I also got a stiff neck looking up at the huge skyscrapers that were being erected along the street. May I give them a nickname? The Ugly Sisters. These monstrosities loom threateningly over much of the old banking district and, in comparison, make the giant glass building behind Milton Keynes railway station look aesthetically pleasing. Until seeing Bishopsgate I had put this eyesore at the top of the "most uninspiringly ugly" list. Sadly, the Bishopsgate buildings prove that some architects have a total lack of humour or appreciation of beauty.

Walking north along the A10 I passed the Geffrye Museum of British Homes and Gardens. Unfortunately, I could not go in as it closed in January 2018 for a two-year, £18 million refurbishment. When having a new kitchen designed and installed in the house in Egerton I also used a builder who charged the earth and took ages. Those three years that I lived in Egerton were among the happiest of my life; they were the first three years of my marriage and of Claire's life. When we left this idyllic home it coincided with my most stressful time at work. Unfortunately, being a person who is not very open with emotions, I bottled up this stress and focussed on work and stopped working on my marriage. I don't dwell on it, I am just thankful for the great times and memories.

Passing swiftly along the usual parades of shops and offices, the A10 veered to the west so I kept going straight on, following the line of Ermine Street, and arrived at the building site that will be the new Tottenham Hotspur football stadium. I counted nine huge cranes that were being used to help erect what looked like a giant modern day amphitheatre. It is being built on the same space as the old ground; so not too far to relocate for fans, memories and ghosts from previous eras. Talking of ghosts and things that go bump in the night, in the 17th century the villagers of Edmonton (the next area of London that I walked through) accused an old woman of being a witch. She was executed at Tyburn, close to Marble Arch in London, scene of many executions of criminals and traitors. Edmonton in Canada gets its name from the fact that the director of the Hudson's Bay Company, James Lake, lived in Edmonton, England.

On passing under the North Circular Road I made my way to Ponders End, the planned stop for the night. Much to my disappointment, the hotel was another C and C. I had not gone quite far enough north. In the morning I took a slight detour and wandered down towards the Lea valley. And I am mighty glad that I did. It was so picturesque. Firstly, I came across the River Lea

Navigation canal, next was the William Girling reservoir and finally I reached the river Lea itself. Having said all that, the Lea valley is one of the flattest that I have ever seen. It would not be until I reached Ware that the Lea valley would earn the right to be called a proper valley with gradients on either side of the waterway.

The canal and its lock brought back wonderful memories I have of two canal holidays, both on the magnificent Llangollen canal. The first one was a week with five fellow post graduate students. One morning we awoke to the shouts of irate bargees. Unaware of what all the fuss was about, we opened the curtains to find the barge floating gently down-stream; yes, canals do have a slight flow even though they are built on the level, must be something to do with locks filling and emptying. Our craft was blocking the waterway. Once we had gained control of the errant vessel it was time to blame the idiot responsible. Unfortunately, no-one could remember who had tied her up the night before. To be more precise, no-one could remember if anyone had tied her up the night before. Then again, it was a rather boozy week. The second holiday on the canal was an altogether different affair. I spent a serene week with my parents and got great delight in seeing Mum steering (she has never learnt to drive a car) and Dad negotiating the locks. Neither of them wanted to be at the helm when we negotiated the precipitous Pontcysyllte aqueduct (the highest in the world) that spans way above the river Dee. One side of the aqueduct had a tow path. The other had nothing to stop you falling to oblivion. Basically, the barge moved along an elongated water filled pig's trough.

My northerly course involved sandwiching me between the manic A10 to the west and the tranquil Lea Valley to the east. First stop, Waltham Cross, just north of the M25. Here I saw the Eleanor cross. Eleanor of Castile was a woman who loved and was much loved by her husband, Edward I. Though the marriage started out as a political alliance, it grew into something far deeper. She even went with him on a crusade to Acre. When she died near Lincoln her body was moved to Westminster Abbey for burial. Edward decreed that a stone cross should be erected at every overnight stop along the way.

Twelve such ornate crosses were erected, of which only three have much of the original stonework intact (Geddington and Hardingstone in Northamptonshire, and Waltham Cross). The final one was at Charing Cross in central London. Beware, the Victorian version now standing there is not a faithful replica of what the original cross looked like. Not that you could accuse me of being a whinger, but I thought that the siting of the Eleanor Cross was all wrong. Yes, I know that it was there long before the modern

Waltham Cross was built. However, the town planners could have made the area around the Cross more in keeping with the ancient monument. Imagine Stonehenge having a shopping mall built all around it and you get the picture.

Without any obvious border, Waltham Cross changed effortlessly into Cheshunt, idyllically situated on the west side of the Lea valley. In "The Domesday Book" (page 137) it says,

> "Cheshunt: Cestrehont/hunt; Count Alan, before and after 1066. Mill, Town with the Waltham Cross ... Cheshunt Great House was the home of Cardinal Wolsey."

The name Cestre suggests that a Roman fort was established here. There is no trace of it now nor that of Cheshunt Great House. With regards to the latter building, it was built in the 15th century, home to Cardinal Wolsey for a while, was owned by freemasons in the 19th century, and then became a museum. During WW2 it was occupied by the Home Guard and later described by locals as the ugliest house in the district. The locals should have seen some of the monstrosities that have been erected in parts of London in later years. In 1965 a mysterious fire finally put the "ugliest house" out of its misery. Six hundred years of history came to a rapid end following this allegedly deliberate fire.

With no Roman fort nor Great House to look for there was a landmark that I wanted to find in Cheshunt; one of the golden post boxes. What, I hear you ask? Following the 2012 Olympic Games, held in England, the Post Office repainted some of its red boxes in honour of those British athletes who achieved gold medals. Native of Cheshunt, Laura Kenny (nee Trott), has the distinction of being the greatest British Olympian with four gold medals, all in track cycling (2012 and 2016 Olympics). The Post Office painted a box in Harlow in her honour and then it was pointed out that she actually was a native of Cheshunt. So they painted one here near the Old Pond fountain in the town centre, but left the golden one in Harlow too I am pleased to say. And one other local celebrity of note; there is a block of retirement flats in Cheshunt called Cliff Richard Court. No, the singer has not retired there. During the 1950s, Harry Webb, the now national treasure Cliff Richard, lived in Cheshunt and went to the secondary school there.

I continued along the route of Ermine Street to Ware for my overnight stop at Fanhams Hall, a grade II listed Jacobean mansion house. Well, sometimes you have to slum it for the sake of your art. This hotel cum conference centre a mile from Ware centre is set amidst verdant countryside. Japanese gardeners were employed to create the hotel's formal gardens. Yippee, no more C and Cs (cheapish and cheerless hotels, remember?).

In the morning, after a belt bursting breakfast (including the best scrambled eggs I have ever tasted), I strolled around the hotel gardens in the spring sunshine and, eventually forcing myself out of my post breakfast laziness, continued on with my walk. Wandering aimlessly around Ware it struck me what a lovely little town it is; clean, uncluttered and no tall buildings to hem you in. It also benefits from having the river Lea run through it. The river had been going north since its parting from the Thames and in Ware it changed direction to the west. I too meandered westwards along the side of the river on what looked like a tow path, eventually coming to a large weir and lock with a couple of canal barges waiting to pass through. The river Lea was the first river that I had come across that doubles up as a canal. Apparently the weir (from which the town gets its name) was built to stop the Vikings from using the navigable river to escape from Alfred the Great.

I wandered past a row of old gazebos (and a couple of nosy swans) along the river's edge.

Apparently, the well to do ladies would sit here whilst their husbands involved themselves in manly pursuits (mainly drinking). Talking of manly pursuits, I also came across a couple of great crested grebes going through what looked like their mating ritual.

Not only is modern day Ware pleasing to the eye, it also has much history to interest the visitor. The Romans had a settlement here. In the tiny museum (run by knowledgeable and enthusiastic volunteers) I saw the skeletal remains of a young girl called Flavia in a lead coffin dating from the Roman period. Based on the material used for her coffin, Flavia probably came from a well to do family. In the floor of one of the rooms was the old well that was the source of water for the nearby priory. An exhibition displayed Ware's association with malting and brewing. The river would have made transporting of barley and beer fairly easy. Opposite the museum a statue commemorating this association was erected. At first I could not understand why the statue has a cat as well as a worker from the maltings (see below). It was one of the museum volunteers who pointed out the blindingly obvious. Barley grains would have attracted rats and mice, so cats were an integral part of the workforce.

There was also a display dedicated to the history of pharmaceuticals made in the town. The global company, Glaxo Smith Klein, is based in Ware. The original line of Ermine Street runs right through the factory.

On retracing my steps back to the town centre I waved farewell to the Lea valley as my way was inexorably north. I would certainly recommend the area as a tourist attraction. As well as the pretty town of Ware it has the river, canal and flooded gravel pits. It was even used in the 2012 Olympics as the site of the canoeing competitions.

Between Ware and Puckeridge I passed through various tiny hamlets (when does a hamlet become a village and a village a town?) that have benefited from the building of the A10 bypass that runs parallel to the road I walked on; first Thundridge, then Wadesmill, up the hill to High Cross and finally Colliers End. Wadesmill is the place where the first turnpike in England, and probably the world, was set up in 1663. Taxes levied were supposed to fund repair of the road which had deteriorated due to the heavy goods vehicles of the day trundling to the maltings in Ware. Those who could, avoided paying the toll by the simple expedient of finding an alternative route (via the Great North Road, for example). Colliers end was tiny and yet according to Herfordshire-genealogy.co.uk,

> "Colliers End is one of the many hamlets which developed along a main road radiating out from London, in this case the London to Cambridge road. In 1882 it had 7 pubs or beer houses, a blacksmith, a wheelwright and a hay and straw dealer to cater for the passing traffic."

The web site also contains some evocative photographs of bygone days. Peruse it at your leisure.

From High Cross to Puckeridge I noticed that I was on a road actually called Ermine Street, and I liked that very much. Less than half a mile north of Puckeridge is the village of Braughing (pronounced Braffing according to Margary). Between Puckeridge and Braughing (at Wickham Hill) evidence of Celtic and Roman settlements has been unearthed. This was the spaghetti junction of its day. Major Roman roads, Ermine Street and Stane Street, crossed here. Even in Celtic times it was a major intersection. From here you could go east to Colchester, west to Biggleswade, southwest to St Albans, northeast to Cambridge and, of course, north along Ermine Street to Lincoln.

One could quite easily miss the village of Braughing, or just assume it is a line of nondescript houses and a pub on the way north from Puckeridge. By the side of the pub, the Golden Fleece (more of that later), is a small footpath that descends to the tiny river Quin. On the other side of the river is the church of St Mary, the Virgin, a beautiful grade I listed building. Carrying on past the church you come to the village proper and a series of wonderful old houses. For cars to get to the village they need to use a ford to cross the river Quin. Despite this area having been a major Roman/Celtic crossroads I could find no suitable hotel so I needed to hop on a bus back to Ware (thank goodness for my free bus pass) and stay another night at Fanhams Hall. I needed to make sure that I didn't get used to staying in such pleasantly situated accommodation.

It was at this point that I had an altogether surreal experience. The bus stop for my return journey from Braughing to Ware was next to the Golden Fleece pub. The buses run every two hours so having an hour to kill, I decided to pop into the pub for a pot of tea. The car park was full so I expected to see a packed pub with lots of local conversations. On entering I noticed that the place was empty apart from a lone biker sitting in one corner of the bar (not a Hell's Angels you understand, but a pedal cyclist). The barwoman was standing idly behind the bar. I ordered my pot of tea and sat down by the open fire. Ten minutes later I went back to the bar and asked if my tea was on its way. The barmaid said that she had forgotten about my order despite me being her only customer. As my tea arrived so did thirty people through the front door. They all lined up in single file and one by one ordered their drinks. The queue was so long that it went out of the door and next to the bus stop. Whilst they were being served around twenty cyclists entered through the rear door and queued up for drinks. The thirty thirsty drinkers were members of Royston Ramblers. They had arrived at the pub earlier in the day, parked their cars, and had gone on a hike. I chatted to two of their number, Peter and Mike. They said that they had just completed a six mile walk. They noticed my rucksack and asked me what I was doing. With a degree of pride (or was it one-upmanship?) I said that I was walking Ermine Street from London to York. We exchanged walkers' stories for half an hour until I realised that my bus was due.

My bus ride from Braughing to Ware was uneventful apart from a minor skirmish at Puckeridge. The bus was a small single decker yet it still struggled to get through the narrow roads, especially when cars were parked on one side. As we passed along one such crowded street I noticed a vehicle pull out of a side road and approach from the opposite direction. The driver of this hulk was the "I've got an off road vehicle so get the f**k out of my way" type. The bus driver, who was there first I have to admit, politely said that he had passengers on board (me and one other person) and so he could not reverse. A stand-off ensued. From the safety of my seat I gave my driver silent encouragement. Three minutes later the car driver edged onto the pavement and the bus just managed to pass. As the vehicles crossed the car driver demonstrated his lack of brain power and limited but colourful use of the English language and in return I gave him my best "lucky you didn't mess with me" stare. He lifted his right hand towards me and gestured that this had happened twice to him already that day.

9 BRAUGHING TO CHESTERTON

Route: Margary 2b (pages 204-207).

In the morning I got the bus from Ware back to Braughing (pronounced Braffing, don't forget) and carried on my journey northwards on foot. As with the stretch from London to Braughing, Ermine Street and the A10 intertwine and overlap all the way to Royston. The Roman road is then the long straight A1198 to Godmanchester. A further couple of miles north at Alconbury, all the way to Chesterton the A1(M) and A1 seem to have been built on top of the Roman road. For this chapter creative route planning was now required to keep me not too far off the straight and narrow. The first part of my journey involved one of these detours; getting to Buntingford via Hare Street, a tiny hamlet built around a crossroad. Before passing through Buntingford I stopped for a brew in the village pub in Westmill, the Sword Inn Hand. Like many buildings I had come across in Hertfordshire, the pub was vividly painted in pink. I spent some time chatting to a couple of the locals, and explained that I was looking forward to walking to Chipping to see the site of its world famous competition which they had never heard of.

In Buntingford I walked along Station road but there was no sign of a station. Sadly the railway line that was opened in 1863 saw its last passengers in 1964 and the final freight trains the following year. The branch line ran from St Margaret's, south of Ware, to Buntingford, a total of 13.8 miles, all of it through rural areas. Lack of freight and falling passenger numbers made it a prime target for closure when the infamous Beeching plans were put together. In "The Reshaping of British Railways (1963)" 55% of stations and 30% of route miles were identified for closure. In "The

Development of the Major Railway Trunk Routes (1965)" only 3,000 miles of the existing 7,500 freight trunk miles would get future investment. Something drastic was needed, it has to be said. In 1962 the railways lost £104 million (equivalent to over £2.1 billion in 2018) of public money. Whether the level of cuts was too drastic is a debating point that finer financial and sociological minds than mine may be able to answer.

On the subject of closed railway lines and business cases, I would just like to mention the Waverley Route (named after the Sir Walter Scott novels that were based in the area). Each year I spend an idyllic holiday in the Scottish Borders with members of my family; the scenery and people are lovely. The Waverley Route was a line that ran from Edinburgh to Carlisle, passing through many Borders towns along the way. In 1849 the Edinburgh to Hawick section opened with the last link to Carlisle being completed in 1862. It must have been one of the most picturesque routes in the network. It fell to the Beeching axe in 1969. In the early 21st century plans were put together to reinstate 30 miles of the line from Edinburgh to Tweedbank (the station lying between the towns of Galashiels and Melrose). Opponents to the scheme in their business case said that only 70 passengers a day would use the route from Galashiels. The line opened in 2015 and the car park at Tweedbank station had to be quickly extended from the original 235 spaces. Trains on the single track line are often overcrowded. Tourism has increased in the area. A mini housing boom has occurred along the route. Finer financial and sociological minds than mine may be able to make sense of that lot.

As a child I do remember walking to Baguley station with my Dad to watch the steam trains racing through the station. To me they were both awesome and frightening in equal measure. When visiting my grandparents I had to walk under a railway bridge. I say walk, but I always ran as fast as I could because I was frightened that a train would pass overhead with me below. Fear can be quite irrational. Just watch me jump if I see a house spider crawling across the carpet.

From Buntingford I walked along a road called Ermine Street and then joined the A10 which had a footpath running alongside it. Here it was long, straight and very flat for virtually the whole of the eight miles to Royston. Three miles out of Buntingford I passed through Chipping. Sadly, it was too early in the year for me to attend the annual "World Sausage Tossing Championship", held at the Countryman Inn at the end of May. The reader will probably already know the rules, but in case you have forgotten them I will elaborate. We are looking at accuracy here, not distance. After all, anyone can throw a sausage. A throne (toilet) is placed in the centre of the arena (field). A competitor (silly hat optional) throws their sausage at the throne. If they get it in the bowl then they have another go.

The winner is the person who gets the most consecutive direct hits. If you miss you pay for your sausage, all proceeds going to charity. People come from near and far for the day long jamboree. In the evening at the event in 2017 the Nashville Teens, a famous rock band with a big hit in the 1960s (Tobacco Road), performed. This year it was John Otway headlining the evening's shindig.

About a mile out of Chipping I became bored with the long, straight, and flat A10 so took a left turn and headed for Therfield. Although there is not much to show for it now, this village has been around for a long time. The ancient track, the Icknield Way, is thought to have run through it. However, there is some debate as to the actual route. In the 13th century map, Scema Britannie, it is shown as a straight line running roughly from Salisbury to Bury St Edmunds, following the chalk ridges of the Berkshire Downs and the Chiltern Hills. A hundred years later the route of Icknield Way had miraculously changed, going from Winchester to Tynemouth via Birmingham. This second suggestion takes the path nowhere near Therfield so I will plum for the first for a reason no more scientific than I happened to be in Therfield and not Birmingham.

Continuing along the quiet country lane I ended up in Royston, another place that the Icknield Way passes through (in an east west direction). Something else that passes through, in a north south alignment, is the Greenwich meridian. Royston attracted both James I and his son, Charles I. The former had a hunting lodge built and then prohibited anyone from catching game within sixteen miles of Royston. Charles was a less frequent visitor and his last visit to Royston was under less happy circumstances. In 1647 the Parliamentary army brought him through the town on the way to London and eventual execution. I stopped in Royston for the night.

The next stage of my journey would be easy to navigate, two days walking along the A1198 to Godmanchester. This section really did feel like I was retracing the steps of the Ninth Legion along Ermine Street. The engineers would have enjoyed building this section, long, straight and flat plus well-drained soil. With pleasant spring weather to accompany me, I was looking forward to this section. On the first day I was treated kindly by the weather and slowed my pace to almost a crawl. I was also treated to another example of the quirky, almost surreal, nature of the rural English. In comparison, Chipping and its sausage tossing competition became a sensible everyday occurrence.

Just out of Royston I passed into Cambridgeshire and noticed a cluster of Paintball venues. A little further on, I came across another cluster, but this time of tiny villages: Kneesworth, Bassingbourn and Whaddon Gap. I allowed myself time to wander around each. On the outskirts of Whaddon Gap is the old RAF station of Bassingbourn. It was first used in 1938 as a training base. During WWII it was upgraded and some of the aircraft involved in the 1,000 bomber raid on Cologne in May 1942 took off from here. It then became home to a section of the United States Army Air Force. Filming also took place here, both during and after the war. Movies like Memphis Belle (documentary), Chain Lightning (Humphrey Bogart) and The Dam Busters (Michael Redgrave) used the location for some of the scenes. Even legendary screen idol Clark Gable was based at Bassingbourn during filming. In 1969 it was turned over to the British Army for use as a training location. In 2012 the former RAF station was then mothballed. As I stared out across the abandoned tranquil airfield I found it impossible to imagine its involvement in the world's most devastating conflict.

The area was also known for coprolite. In the 19th century huge amounts of fossilised dung were dug up in the fields, ground down and used as a fertiliser. Now here comes the surreal bit. In

2005, to celebrate their past, £10,000 was made available to the locals. They voted on three suggestions. The first, a statue of a heron, was thought too flimsy. The second, a representation of a WWII bomber was too obvious. The third suggestion was the clear winner; in celebration of the importance of coprolite to the local economy a statue of "a heap of muck on top of a plinth" (in the words of the artist who designed the monument, David Billings) would be commissioned. Sadly, I found no evidence of the statue in my wanderings.

Taking advantage of the balmy weather, I then strolled towards Wimpole Hall, the largest house in Cambridgeshire. About half a mile from the hall the heavens opened up and I quickly put on my wet weather gear. By the time I had reached the venue there were puddles everywhere. When I entered the hall I was asked to put on a pair of blue polythene galoshes to help protect the carpets (I call them Noddy shoes). To my embarrassment, I was unable to cover my right boot; I have an arthritic hip and my right leg does not bend as well as it should. The man at the door shod me as if I were an old horse. Whilst doing the honours he asked me where I had come from. During our conversation I mentioned that I had stopped for a brew at the brightly coloured pub at Westmill. I said that vivid colours seemed to be the norm and added that the beautiful thatched cottage opposite the pub was painted bright blue. He said that I was talking about his house – it's a small world.

This National Trust property and estate is well worth a visit. The author Rudyard Kipling's daughter Elsie and her husband, George Bambridge, were the last owners of the hall. On her death in 1976 she bequeathed it to the National Trust. I found one room, the breakfast room, extremely moving. Prior to Bambridge's death in 1943 the couple had used the large dining room to entertain guests. When he died Elsie converted it into a kitchen and used the adjoining room to take her meals. The table in this room was small. It was as if she no longer wished to entertain visitors. I got the feeling that for the last 30 years of her life, Elsie lived a lonely existence, with only servants and memories to keep her company. There is an extensive library at the hall and the tour around the servants' quarters demonstrated the stark contrast between life above and below stairs. In the basement there was a huge plunge pool which probably got little or no use after Bambridge's death. In the bathroom next to Elsie's bedroom there used to be a vivid pink 1960's style bath. The National Trust had this removed as they felt that it was not in keeping with the rest of the surroundings.

The overcast skies suggested that the rain was here to stay for some time so I bit the bullet and left the comfort of the hall and continued towards Caxton. Just before reaching Caxton, I noticed a sign to the right for Bourn Hall. This is where the world's first IVF test tube baby, Louise Brown, was conceived, so to speak, in 1978. To the east of Caxton lies the totally new parish/hamlet/village/town of Cambourne. I'm not too sure what to call it as even as I write the place is expanding substantially. If I had looked out from Caxton in 1997 there would only have been farmland to see. Now it is an ever spreading sea of streets and houses, part of the government's plan to build many thousands of new homes in the southeast. An unusually high birth rate in the area (nothing to do with Bourn Hall) is also contributing to a dramatic rise in population.

And then I arrived at Papworth Everard, home to Papworth hospital. The year after Louise Brown was conceived a short distance away at Bourn Hall, Papworth was the scene of the first successful British heart transplant operation. Nine years later, in 1986, surgeons performed the world's first triple transplant operation there. Davina Thompson received a new heart, lung and liver. And how did the place get such an unusual name? A couple of hundred years after the Romans left Britain, a local Saxon leader called Papa established a settlement in the area. Papworth means "the enclosure of Papa's people". After the Norman Conquest, the knight Everard de Beche was granted the village and adjoining land.

Having stayed the night in Papworth Everard, I awoke to continuing inclement weather. Unfortunately, the gently warming south-westerly drizzle of the previous day had become a wet and gusty, northerly one, driving the stinging rain into my face. Within five minutes of starting off from Papworth Everard I was cold, wet, weary and thoroughly fed up. It was six miles to Godmanchester, and there were no towns or villages between, only the B1044 and fields. I did what any self-respecting rambler would do in the circumstances and turned back and found a tea shop. Actually it was the Garden Restaurant, the café attached to the hospital. I hopped in there and after leaving a puddle at the counter, devoured a steaming mug of tea and a flapjack (I love flapjacks). Here, I was informed that the hospital would soon be closing for good and the facilities moved to a new building in Cambridge.

Whilst in the hospital café, I could not help but remember the times I used to go with my ex-wife to Christies Hospital in Manchester; times that I felt utterly useless. She had found a lump in one of her breasts and was soon after diagnosed with cancer. The treatment was long and painful but, combined with her strength of character, eventually successful. Like the time of our daughter's birth, all I could do was offer moral support. How different to my previous visits to Christies as a post graduate student conducting research into the effects of radiation on the enzyme carbonic anhydrase. It is because of the need for continual research to help fight against cancer that half of my royalties will be donated to Cancer Research UK. This is a disease that affects old and young alike and can be a rapidly or chronically fatal illness. Great strides have been made in recent years and the prognosis in many cases is excellent thanks to the valuable work that the cancer charities undertake.

Following my tea and flapjack I was ready to march on to Godmanchester. Poking my nose outside, I noticed that it was still raining heavily so I hopped on a bus instead. The fifteen minutes bus journey was along the same road that I would have walked anyway and it was just one field after another for the six miles. So I didn't miss anything.

The name Godmanchester, Roman name Durovigutum, suggests that it was the site of a Roman fortified camp. This was a prime site to base troops, being by the River Great Ouse and at the crossroads of three important Roman arteries (Ermine Street from London to York, the Via Devana linking Colchester to Chester, and a military road from Sandy in Bedfordshire). Despite the rain I forced myself to walk to the riverside and the Chinese Bridge, a small white structure that led to a water meadow. The current bridge replaced the old one in 2010. The earlier one was alleged to have been built without nails or fixings. Before I walked onto the new one I did a cursory check and it seemed secure enough to take my weight. The rain was bouncing off the river.

From Godmanchester I made my way under the A14 dual carriageway, across a footbridge and into Huntingdon. As I walked across the footbridge wobbled noticeably. Until the building of the bypass in 1974, the road bridge that runs alongside the footbridge was the only available crossing of the Great Ouse in the vicinity of the town. Traffic, pedestrians and vehicles of all sizes, would have had to share the space, regardless of any health and safety issues. Having said that, there are parapets on the bridge which allowed pedestrians to retreat into when larger trucks were crossing. Built in the 14th century and still going strong, construction was started on both sides of the river at the same time. Engineers did not quite get the alignment right so there is a slight kink in the centre of the bridge.

Two of the nation's former leaders were members of parliament for Huntingdon; Oliver Cromwell and John Major. In fact, this is where Cromwell was born. For education purposes, and not to keep out of the rain, I visited the Cromwell Museum, sited on High Street in the old grammar school building. It was an hour well spent. Close by I noticed two war memorials. The first was in honour of the town's dead of the first and second world wars. I was taken by surprise when I read what was on the second one. This is the only Boer War memorial that I have ever seen. It listed the names of 38 Huntingdonshire men who lost their lives during the war in South Africa from 1899 to 1902.

High Street changed to Ermine Street and I was quickly out of Huntingdon, aiming towards the A1M. Oblivious to the rain, I strode along Ermine Street; I suppose once you have got wet through, a few more drops don't matter. I squelched through Great Stukeley and dripped into Little Stukeley. This is the village that was the backdrop for RAF Alconbury. From here RAF Bomber Command and then the USAAF launched missions during WWII. In more recent times USAAF A-10's (affectionately known as warthogs) based there were used in the Gulf war of 1991. It is now a tactical support centre. I stopped at a small B and B for the night, grateful for the opportunity to take off my wet weather gear.

Suitably dried out and filled with a typical full English breakfast, I met the mighty A1M, a mile north of Little Stukeley. This would be my constant companion throughout the day as my route would run parallel with it, and no more than a hundred yards from it, for the next fourteen miles, all the way to Chesterton.

***

It was whilst I was walking on this stretch of my journey that a couple of thoughts struck me. Firstly, the A1M was busy and noisy, and I mean really noisy. Secondly, Ermine Street goes through a lot of empty space. Since passing under the M25 near Waltham Cross I had not come upon any major town of note apart from Ware (sorry Royston) nor seen evidence of thriving industries. In fact, after London, I would only come across two cities along the entire length of Ermine Street; Lincoln and York. I may not be passing through many towns along my route but there certainly are a lot out there.

The growth of towns throughout the world has been phenomenal. At the start of the 19th century, only 3% of the global population lived in cities. By the beginning of the 21st century this had risen to nearly 50%. How do we explain this? I am not a social historian but my simple explanation is as follows. Hunter gatherers followed their food supply and so there was little need to put down roots. With the development of agriculture a base had to be established; a nomadic existence was seen as a less attractive and more risky proposition. Adding the need for security to regular supplies of clean water, food and fuel meant that small communities began to grow. Trading of surpluses and shortages linked settlements. Over time (and perhaps coinciding with a realisation of the importance of habitat management and conservation) self-awareness and a sense of self-importance developed. With this development of self and higher thinking, and an inability to understand and explain the world around them, people created religion, art and hierarchy. These, with their various forms of glorification, generated cultures of haves and have nots, leaders and followers. Wealth creation and the accumulation of items accorded high value and status (but no obvious practical value) became ends in themselves rather than a way of ensuring that day to day needs could be met. Wealth creators, let's call them industrialists, throughout the ages have sought economies of scale, increased efficiency and a ready supply of raw materials, energy and people from outlying areas to drive their profits. Attracting people into an area meant the destruction of some communities and the development of others into towns. The boom towns in the USA gold rush days are classic examples of rapid urban growth and decay. When the gold ran out so did the prospectors and associated ancillary workers. Transport links were key to urban growth; back to logistics and getting products to the right place at the lowest cost. As I walked along Ermine Street it was obvious that farming was the number one industry. Even tourism is only a very minor consideration. Maybe if the bottom had not fallen out of the coprolite market the village of Bassingbourn would have become a city.

Let us now consider Roman towns in Britain in particular. On the Continent, the Roman expansion went into areas with already clearly defined centres of administration and population. However, in Britain centres like Colchester were few and far between. Some of these urban areas were the bases of future client kings like Togidubnus (Silchester, Winchester and Chichester all being within his sphere of control). Although there is some archaeological evidence of late Iron Age presence at the sites of future Roman towns, the island was basically a collection of small communities whose main motive was survival and primary industry was agriculture. That there is overlap between Iron Age and Roman locations should be of little surprise; availability of water, food and fuel would be seen as prerequisites for both. There would also have been some overlap in the road and track networks for the efficient military control and civil administration.

Had the Romans not invaded Britain then the urbanisation process would have continued, albeit at a slower pace. As it is, historians have only identified 24 places that we would recognise as major Roman towns. David Mattingly, in "An Imperial Possession, Britain in the Roman Empire", lists them on pages 268-269. These are split into three hierarchical types; coloniae, municipia and civitas centres.

There were up to five coloniae; Colchester, Lincoln, Gloucester, York and probably London. The first three were founded on territory that had been conquered and where retired army veterans were granted land along with their pension. If you were a citizen of a colonia then you were a Roman citizen with rights throughout the Empire. Non-citizens, the incolae, would have been seen as second class. Coloniae were the highest status towns in the Roman Empire and subject to Roman law and its constitution. Some were exempt from paying taxes. York successfully petitioned to change from a municipium to a colonia. It is thought that London also successfully petitioned.

The second class of Roman town was the municipia, of which St Albans was the only one in Britain. Municipia tended to be important tribal centres that had been conquered. There were a number of Roman citizens along with the indigenous population. Roman laws were obligatory.

The civitas centre was the chief town of an area or tribe and often the base of a client king. The ancient names of some of these towns indicate the tribal centres. Prasutagus, client king of the

Iceni, was based in the civitas known as Venta Icenorum (Caister-by-Norwich). The administration centre for the defeated Silures tribe of Wales was known as Venta Silurum. I had already visited one civitas on my walk, Durnovernum Cantiacorum (Canterbury), the centre for the Cantiaci tribe. Shortly I would visit another, Durobrivae (Water Newton) and later on Petuaria Parisiorum (Brough-on-Humber). Local laws would have been in operation in these places.

Not only the laws and administration of Roman towns would have seemed alien to the Celts. Americans, used to their grid system, transported back in time to a Roman town would have felt more at home than the conquered Britons. Straight roads crossed at right-angles creating regular building plots. These rectangular areas, known as insulae, were where the rectangular shops, houses and other buildings were erected. In "What the Romans Did for Us" (page 101), Philip Wilkinson says,

> "This would have looked strikingly new in a Britain in which many houses were round and in which most settlements grew organically with little or nothing in the way of a master plan. Roman towns would have looked much more regimented and ordered than earlier British settlements."

Although the exact types of building in a Roman town would depend on its size, there were a number of common structures. At the heart was the forum, a large rectangular open space surrounded on three sides by a covered walkway and on the fourth by the basilica. This building was often the largest one in town and it acted as the administration (equivalent to a modern town hall) and judicial (law courts) centres. The three other sides would contain shops and eating houses. In the open space in the centre people could meet and chill out. Many modern day public squares are based on this Roman design. There would have been a mansio, a large building that acted as a hotel for visiting officials and officers of the army and as the focal point of the Roman postal service. The square temples tended to be small, far less grand than our cathedrals. Here people could make offerings rather than gather for large scale communal worship, which took place in the open space around the temples.

And then the towns would contain the houses, some of which doubled up as shops too. Well to do people had gardens incorporated into the designs and maybe hypocausts to provide under floor heating. More often people had to be content with open fires or braziers. Those who could afford the luxury of glass built windows which kept the heat in. The Celts did not have windows, just holes in walls covered with cloth to act as doors. As ground space became limited, people who could afford extensions built upwards. Most of the houses were crammed tightly together. As they were generally made of wood, fire was an ever present hazard. Many houses did not have kitchens so the risk of fire would have come from the braziers and small candles used as lighting. Incidentally, the Romans are credited with developing candles with wicks in.

Some towns had amphitheatres, where theatrical productions and tournaments were staged. These tended to be on a less grand scale than their continental counterparts, but even so some could accommodate a few thousand spectators. During my research I was disappointed to find out that archaeologists have so far not unearthed any evidence of circuses (racetracks for chariots) in Britain, despite the Romans love of horses and the Celts fondness for war chariots.

Outside the town limits the Romans introduced Britain to villas. These were primarily farms that grew into country estates; gentleman farmers grew rich supplying the agricultural needs of the rapidly increasing population. Affluent Britons, keen to emulate their masters, also became proud owners of these desirable residences. Many had exquisitely tiled mosaic floors and walls and their own baths. Wilkinson (page 115) says,

> "Roman villas could be houses of great sophistication and luxury. Even the simplest villas were a far cry from anything built by the native Britons. The most basic features, such as separate rooms and corridors, gave a sense of privacy quite unknown in the simple, one-room houses of the Celts."

The Romans not lucky enough to own their own villas liked to keep clean too. Towns would have had bath houses and public lavatories and thus a ready water supply. In Britain we are blessed with a temperate climate with only extremely rare occasions when water has to be rationed in some areas. Rivers, streams and springs negated the need for the building of major aqueducts that were required in the warmer areas of the Empire. Even so, the water had to be piped to the right places. As Wilkinson says (page 108),

> "Roman Britain had nothing on the scale of the vast aqueducts of France and Spain, but archaeologists have unearthed the remains of water-supply systems at many British sites. The longest was at Lincoln, where some thirty-two kilometres of earthenware supply pipes have been found."

Less healthy lead pipes have also been unearthed at some sites. Where fresh water came in so waste water and effluent had to go out. Often the waste water from the bath houses was used to flush the effluent away in the sewers. Before the Romans arrived sanitary systems were rudimentary at best. Sadly, when the Romans left Britain the locals did not value their sewage systems and most fell into disrepair. Well into the middle of the 19th century diseases due to poor sanitary conditions were rife in Britain, killing many thousands of people. It took an act of parliament to put into law what the Romans had taken for granted. In 1848 the Public Health Act meant that there had to be some form of sanitary arrangement in each house, but not necessarily a flushing toilet.

Some of the towns on Mattingly's list have grown substantially since Roman times (London, Leicester, Carlisle) but others have become quiet villages with substantial Roman ruins (Wroxeter) or just sleepy hollows with no evidence of their previous Roman glory (Water Newton). When the last of the Roman conquerors departed in AD410 so did the reason for the existence of some of their towns. Having said all that, of the 24 Roman towns in England and Wales listed by Mattingly, I would have visited 7 by the end of my ramble; not a bad hit rate considering I was only following in the Ninth Legion's footsteps.

Whatever the reasons for urban growth and decay, Roman or otherwise, the role of Ermine Street has changed from being one of Britain's most important roads linking military and administration centres to just the approximate route of a major artery that supplies the raw materials and people that fuel the towns and cities elsewhere. Oh, let's not forget, it is also the route of this intrepid explorer.

***

Back to the walk to Chesterton. Six miles out of Little Stukeley I had my first signs of life; in the village of Sawtry a man was walking his dog. A mile further on, in Stilton, I saw no signs of life at all. Stilton could be used as a role model for the decline of a community. The village grew because Ermine Street and then the Great North Road passed through it. It was a busy coaching stop and it is alleged that at one point there were 14 inns and 500 villagers servicing the needs of the passing trade. This passing trade as well as the pubs all but dried up when the A1 bypass was built in the late 1950s; Stilton being the first section of bypass to be built between London and Newcastle. In an attempt to generate interest in the village an annual cheese rolling race was started in 1962. This event has now been cancelled due to lack of interest, or maybe because some people rolled logs instead of cheese. This is all rather sad when you consider that stilton cheese is, in my opinion, one of the best varieties in the world. There is no definitive proof that the cheese was conceived or ever made in the village. One suggested reason why it got its name was because the coaching inns sold it.

The village does boast an 18 holes golf course that is open to the public. Now I am not a good golfer. In fact, when I moved out of the house in Egerton I left my clubs in the garage and didn't bother to go back for them. My best times on a golf course involved taking my wonderful Labrador, Honey, for walks on the one that was at the back of the house in Lostock. On one ramble she found ten balls. Within a couple of years we had a collection of about 200. Only once did she pick up a live ball, one that was being used during a game. I saw the funny side of it, the golfer didn't. Honey died just before her twelfth birthday. She was my constant companion for those twelve years and brought such joy into my life. I loved that dog.

It is said that golf is a good walk ruined. It was also full of amusing experiences when played with members of my family. On one memorable occasion I was playing with my brother George and brothers-in-law Chris and Stuart. The first and last holes had parallel fairways. At the first I played my tee shot and achieved a creditable (for me anyway) fifty yards. Chris hit a good straight shot of well over 100 yards. George sliced his shot sideways onto the 18th fairway. Stuart took a mighty swing and hit his tee shot with great strength. It would have gone about 200 yards but for the fact that it hit the marker post on the tee and ricocheted backwards. He is the only golfer I know whose second shot started further back than his first. As we advanced along the fairway George crossed to the 18th and played his second shot. It must have gone at least 150 yards. The next thing we knew a very irate golfer rushed over and demanded to know why his ball had been hit back up the fairway to the 18th tee. George had hit the wrong ball. Later in the round Stuart borrowed Chris's new driver. He miss hit his shot so much that the club head separated from the shaft and ended up further up the fairway than the ball. Appreciating that he could never better his performance, Stuart retired from playing golf ever again. Chris sadly let the side down. He took lessons and eventually became captain of his club with a single figure handicap.

Less than a mile from Stilton is Norman Cross. I was expecting big things when I arrived here. After all, the name does have a certain gravitas. All I could see was the A15 leading off the A1M in an easterly direction towards Peterborough. This is the same A15 that I would meet up with later in my journey. If you look at Google Maps you will see that the field to the right of the A1M and on the northern side of the A15 does have some unusual markings on its northern edge. This is all that remains of the site of the world's first purpose built prisoner of war camp that was constructed during the Napoleonic Wars. For seventeen years it housed thousands of POWs (soldiers and sailors), 1770 of whom perishing there. The site was chosen for four reasons. Firstly, it was next to the Great North Road and its link to London. Secondly, Peterborough was close by with an abundance of manpower. Thirdly, the surrounding areas provided a ready supply of food and water. Lastly, the proximity of Yarmouth and King's Lynn meant that ferrying in prisoners was relatively easy. Using the prison camp reduced the reliance on prison ships that were notoriously cramped and disease ridden. Sadly, most of the casualties at Norman Cross were as a result of disease anyway (typhus being the biggest killer, plus smallpox, measles, consumption and dysentery). In 1914, to commemorate the 100th anniversary of the closure of the camp and to honour those who died there, a monument with a bronze eagle on top was erected. In 1990 the eagle was stolen (for scrap perhaps) and it took until 2005 to fund a replacement. So, Norman Cross does have a sense of gravitas after all.

A couple of miles further on I reached Chesterton, but more of that in the next chapter. After a day of solitary walking (I had only seen one man and his dog all day) I was craving the presence of people. So I waved a brief farewell to the A1, popped over to the outskirts of Peterborough, booked into a crowded hotel, ate a curry in a busy Indian restaurant, had a few beers in a packed pub and finished off with what I hoped would be, a quiet and peaceful slumber.

It took me some time to finally drop off to sleep. It wasn't because the hotel was noisy, you understand, because after ten o'clock it was very quiet. I put it down to the fact that every now and then you have one of those nights when it is hard to drop off. Having said that, during the night I had a weird dream that involved playing a game of crazy golf. Instead of a ball I had to hit a Stilton cheese through the obstacles. At the end of the course an eagle stole the cheese. I blame it on the vindaloo.

10 CHESTERTON TO LINCOLN

Route: Margary 2c (pages 224-230).

In the morning I retraced my steps to Chesterton and found a few houses and a church (St Michael). After zigzagging through the country lanes for a few hundred metres, risking life and limb crossing the A1 and scrambling through a dense thicket, I arrived at Water Newton where I found even fewer houses and another church (St Regimus). I was close to the site of military and non-military settlements that eventually became a Roman civitas. Whilst carrying out my research it was apparent that some historians talk about Chesterton and many others about Water Newton when they are referring to the whole area covering both the civilian and military sites. For the sake of simplicity I will call the area Water Newton.

The current hamlet of Water Newton lies on the river Nene. This waterway flows languidly into the Wash (North Sea) close to Kings Lynn. It is navigable as evidenced by the lock I noticed near to the church of St Regimus. In fact you could paddle your canoe all the way from Northampton to the sea (88 miles). Incidentally, if you go 30 miles upstream in the direction of Northampton you will get to Hardwater Mill. And why should I mention that little snippet? Well, our old friend Thomas Becket, archbishop of Canterbury, is alleged to have hidden there in 1164 whilst escaping to France.

With easily navigable access to the sea Water Newton was an ideal place to locate a Roman fort during the Ninth Legion's march north. A useful guide to understanding the siting and size of Roman forts is Paul Bidwell's "Roman Forts in Britain". On page 12 there is a map of Britain showing 298 forts with by far the most crowded area being that along the route of Hadrian's Wall. This list is not exhaustive as Bidwell excludes unproven sites, watch towers and minor, temporary buildings. In simple terms, the more people that needed keeping an eye on the bigger the fort. The further the legions got from the southeast then in general the indigenous population became more thinly spread, with fewer large settlements and little interaction between communities. At the same time army lines of communication and supply were becoming more stretched. In the area I was now walking the Romans built forts separated by a day's march (12 miles). These could control large areas and still maintain good communications. With little risk of attack they could be far smaller than the fortresses that were needed to oversee conquered tribes, as in the case in Colchester.

An army marching into unfamiliar territory, with a potentially hostile horde just over the next hillock, would find a degree of comfort in a hastily erected fort. In "What the Romans Did for Us" (page 38), Philip Wilkinson says,

> "The invasion force needed forts to accommodate their troops as soon as they arrived. These bases needed to be built quickly and in large numbers to consolidate the conquest."

He then describes the building process. For quickness, a standard blueprint was used, using locally sourced earthwork and wood. Surveyors would choose a suitable site and then the task of building began with the digging of a ditch. A rampart, made of earth and stones (depending upon availability), was erected behind the ditch. This could have been up to 3.5 metres high. On top a wooden palisade or fence was constructed and a walkway incorporated to allow defending soldiers to stand. Wooden towers and gatehouses were added. Inside the palisade, the Roman buildings tended to be rectangular, standardised and sited according to predetermined plans. The remnants of the stone forts that we see nowadays are those constructed later in the campaign when there was time to build sturdier permanent bases.

To the Celts, the speed and solidity of construction of the Roman defences would have initially been a shock and then a continuous stark reminder of the efficiency of the imperial power. They had already suffered in battle at the hands of well drilled and well-armed troops. Now they saw that the invaders meant to stay. For most this meant accepting the inevitable and adapting to their presence.

The siting of a military establishment in an area attracted people to it. Soldiers had plenty of ready money to spend and they needed something to spend it on. As communities developed, specific industries grew alongside; the type of industry depending on availability of raw materials and customers. Pottery was a lucrative business if you could win a contract to supply the needs of the many thousands of Roman soldiers. Lindsay Allason-Jones in "Women in Roman Britain" (page 75) says,

> *"Some of the smaller towns were established to provide housing for workers in specific industries. Mancetter, Chesterton and Water Newton, for example, were pottery towns, as was Congresbury, whilst others, such as Braughing* [pronounced Braffing, don't forget]*, were metalworking centres."*

In Martin Millett's book "Roman Britain" (page 66) there is an aerial photograph showing the layout of the civitas of Water Newton with Ermine Street running straight through the centre. If you look closely you can make out the outline. On Google Maps it is roughly the area surrounded by Billing Brook, the river Nene and the A1. Using the satellite view I could see faint traces which I persuaded myself were the lines of old streets.

And how big did the civitas get? The enclosed area of Roman Londinium was 316 acres compared to 45 acres at Water Newton. Although Water Newton is considerably smaller than Londinium, size is not the only indicator of a place's economic importance. This was a major industrial town in its day. In effect, Water Newton became the Roman equivalent of Burslem, Stoke and the Staffordshire potteries of the 19th and 20th century. And when the market for what you make disappears (as all Roman soldiers did by AD410) you end up in the 21st century with a few houses and a church and only archaeological evidence of past glories. Having said that, some of the finds at Water Newton are incredibly impressive. Opposite page 65 of Millett's book there is a colour photograph of Christian silver plate dating from the middle of the 4th century. It is believed that these artefacts are the earliest known Christian church plates in existence. Also found alongside the 28 silver objects were a number of coins from the same era. Water Newton may not have the impressive remains of a walled fortress like Richborough, nor the petrified remains of Pompeii, and not even the baths of Bath, but nowhere else has the distinction of being the site of the oldest Christian plate ever discovered. And I liked the idea of that very much. With that cheery thought I carried on my journey.

***

After a couple of minutes I had a less cheery thought, having realised that to continue along Ermine Street I needed to walk along the A1 which had no path for pedestrians. This would also include scrambling through that dense thicket again to reach the road. So, after consulting my map, I did a lot more zigzagging off the straight and narrow, using footpaths and lanes. And so I saw more of the English countryside and villages than I had originally planned, which was a bonus. From Water Newton I had to cross the river Nene twice; using the lock gates and then a footbridge. As I made my way towards Upton I could hear the constant rumble of traffic from first the A1 and then the A17. In Upton I noticed yet again that here was a tiny village with a few houses and a Norman church (John the Baptist).

I wondered, how many churches did the Normans build in England? Actually, they just carried on the impetus of building parish churches that the late Anglo Saxons had started. Britainexpress.com gives a good potted history of Anglo Saxon and Norman church building. Their article begins evocatively,

> "There are few sights that evoke "Englishness" more than that of a slumbering parish church. Cathedrals in England span only about 400 years of English history and cultural influence (with the exception of a few modern cathedra, which sometimes don't evoke much of anything).
>
> Parish churches, on the other hand, tell the tale of some 1500 years of English history and social change. The humble parish church is an integral part of English social life and culture."

May I take this opportunity to sing the praises of this website? It is easy to navigate and is written by people who have an obvious love of history.

The first parish churches were built by local lords and not the clergy. They were symbols of wealth and status and a commitment to Christianity. Whatever the reason they were built there is no denying that they enrich the landscape and enriched my journey from Richborough to York. Although I do not describe them in much detail in this book I always tried to find time to pop inside the churches I came across. And how many churches are there in England? A staggering 37,500. Having said that there are about 43,600 towns and villages and many of the towns will have numerous places of worship.

***

On leaving Upton I could have taken the line of two Roman roads towards Lincoln. If I had gone due north from Upton I would have followed the very straight King Street which joins with the A15 at Thetford and eventually meets up with Ermine Street at Ancaster. This old Roman road, about 30 miles long, is designated as Margary 26. He describes it thus (page 232),

> *"Although Ermine Street (2c) was evidently the original main thoroughfare from the south to the very important Roman centre at Lincoln, it appears that this second route, running almost due north from Durobrivae* [Water Newton] *to Bourne and thence north-west to rejoin Ermine Street at Ancaster, was also constructed at an early date. Its purpose was perhaps to skirt the Fens more closely and to make contact with the Roman canal, the Car Dyke, which comes very close to it south of Bourne."*

As it was, I veered northwest to Stamford, this being the route of Ermine Street. Within two miles of Upton there are four nature reserves and I passed three of them. The one that I did not see, as it was to the east of my route, was Castor Hanglands national nature reserve. As well as ancient ash and maple woodlands its ponds are home to the great crested newt. Two of the three I did come across were so small that one could drive past without realising they were there. As I was on foot, I was able to see the full extent of each one just by standing by the roadside. First of all was Southorpe Paddock nature reserve, then a short distance away was Southorpe Meadow nature reserve, roughly the size of a football field. The recent rain may have encouraged the local moles into serious activity because the reserve looked like the mole version of a camp site. The last one I came across was much larger and I wandered through it. This was Barnack Hills and Holes national nature reserve. As the name suggests this unusual terrain was a series of small humps and holes; the result of limestone quarrying by Romans, Anglo Saxons and Normans. Both

Peterborough and Ely cathedrals used Barnack limestone in their construction. This last site reminded me of the WWI battlefields that I had seen with their innumerable shell holes. To be honest, I did not see any of the reserves in their full glory as it was too early in the season for the meadow flowers. However, I was grateful for having chanced upon these natural oases in a sea of managed farmland.

Close to the Cambridgeshire/Lincolnshire border I came to the entrance for Burghley House and gardens so went in for a quick look. I knew that Burghley was the place famous for the horse trials but what a majestic Elizabethan building there is too.

Capability Brown, famous landscape designer, is responsible for the layout of part of the estate and also the lake. The house (house seems such a petty name for what is quite palatial) was built for Sir William Cecil, one of Queen Elizabeth I's most senior ministers.

Having done my detour from Water Newton I was now back to the original line of Ermine Street, making my way through Stamford and finally walking across the strangely named river Gwash to Great Casterton. As the name suggests, a Roman fort was built here in AD44 which expanded into a walled town. I then reversed back into Stamford and bed. Stamford, rather than Great Casterton, was chosen by me as there was no suitable accommodation at the latter. Stamford, by the river Welland, was also chosen by the Anglo Saxons and Danes as the preferred site of a town as the Welland was more navigable than the Gwash.

Of all the days that I spent walking (including those places I was still to pass through) I believe that the ramble from Water Newton to Great Casterton was my most enjoyable. It was quite idyllic; walking through tiny villages, popping into old parish churches, crossing gently flowing rivers and streams, seeing nature reserves, visiting a grand country house, wandering through farmland, roaming around what was the site of a Roman civitas, and yes, a short stroll through a small town. I do appreciate that there is far more to England. What makes my country the best place to live is the diversity of landscapes, natural and manmade, and the variety of the pace of life. On the grand scale England is small and this rich diversity can be reached within a short drive. However, I am a country bumpkin at heart and as I lay in bed in my hotel in Stamford I wondered if any of the places I had passed through during the day had a vacancy for a village idiot. And where did I stay the night? At Sir William Cecil's place; sadly, not Burghley house, but the Georgian hotel of the same name. On the outskirts of Stamford is a sign that instructs visitors to "Do Come Again". I will definitely obey this command as both town and surrounding area are rather wonderful.

The following day I took a fifteen minutes detour by train to Oakham and then strolled down to Rutland Water. This strictly was not part of my plan but I have always had an inkling to see Rutland Water, one of the largest man-made lakes in Europe; not bad considering Rutland used to be the smallest county in England. Also it again meant that I could avoid the A1. Whilst in Oakham I visited the castle and I have to admit that from the outside it looked more like a church than a fortification; granted there were the remains of old earthwork ramparts and ditches around the castle.

Inside there was an impressive collection of horseshoes of different sizes. Some were huge. I would hate to come across a horse that they could fit. Apparently any royalty visiting the town for the first time has to donate a horseshoe to the castle. The first one was donated by Edward IV in 1470 following the nearby battle of Losecoat Field during the Wars of the Roses. So the giant horseshoes were more symbolic than practical.

Maybe the tradition came about because in 1180 a Norman baron, Walkelin de Ferrers built the great hall of the castle. His emblem was an upside down horseshoe; linguistic connection between Ferrers and farriers (blacksmiths) perhaps? Or, maybe the locals saw a good way of boosting the tourist trade.

An exhibit in the Castle that I took great delight in fiddling with was a copy of the Bayeux Tapestry. It was in the form of a long scroll wrapped around two wheels with handles that you could turn. For purely scientific purposes you understand, I turned the right hand handle so that I saw the full length of the tapestry. The original is not a tapestry by the way. Apparently it should be called the Bayeux Embroidery. Seeing this record covering events before, during and after the Norman Conquest would be a good link to my visit to Stamford Bridge later in my journey. In Oakham I also saw a set of stocks with five holes in. That must have meant that a person would have been incarcerated with wrists, ankles and neck all in a line – an almost impossible contortion for the average human. It made my arthritic hip twitch just looking at it.

Having wandered down to Rutland Water I realised that, whilst it was on the same scale as its counterparts in the Lake District, here was a genteel lake, surrounded by sleepy, sloping farmland. This was a place where one would have an al fresco lunch of cucumber sandwiches whilst sipping Earl Grey out of china cups. It was not the boisterous, towering hills and crags of Cumbria where a mid-ramble picnic would include doorstep sandwiches and mugs of strong steaming tea whilst cowering behind a stone wall to get shelter from the wind and driving rain. On taking in its panoramic view I felt that Rutland Water was more English than the lakes and mountains of Cumbria, which seemed closer in character to their Celtic cousins of North Wales and the Highlands of Scotland. I was pleased to have made my detour to this stretch of inland water.

Water has always held a fascination for me right from the first time I saw the sea. I was about seven years old and on my first ever family holiday in Abergele, North Wales. We had made the journey from Manchester by train; an experience in itself when parents are contending with luggage and four enthusiastic children. I still remember us all crowding into a compartment designed for six adults. A man was already at his seat, reading. As we trooped in, being hushed by Mum, he looked up, said good morning, and then hid behind his newspaper for the rest of the ride. That holiday, during a cold and sometimes damp Easter week, was wonderful. Learning to skim stones and smelling the ozone-rich sea air for the first time are abiding memories. My brother John and I each got souvenir "Jenny Jones" penknives, about two inches long. I lost mine and John very kindly gave me his; almost sixty years later I still have that penknife in my Mr Benn drawer. Mr Benn was a children's TV cartoon character who went on wonderful adventures by going into a tailor's shop and trying on different costumes in the changing room. When he stepped out he was in a place linked to the costume he was wearing. He always brought something back to help him remember the trip. A wonderfully gentle series from a gentle age.

We had more super family holidays in North Wales and a couple in Morecambe on the Lancashire coast. It was here that I got my first taste of the food of the gods, flapjacks. Here also were the Jumping Jimminies, small trampolines that one could bounce up and down on for ages without getting bored. I did not realise it at the time, but my parents must have had the patience of saints.

***

From Oakham I aimed for Stretton (back on Ermine Street) via Cottesmore for my overnight stop. RAF Cottesmore was home to part of the nation's nuclear deterrent (Victor and Vulcan bombers) and more latterly home to Harrier jump jets. In 2001 it became an army establishment called the Kendrew barracks. Of all the Strettons in England, and there are seventeen in total, only two are not on the routes of Roman roads. This seems spooky until you realise that Stretton actually means "settlement on a Roman road". Unfortunately in this settlement on a Roman road I could not find anywhere to stay so I decided to greet them in Greetham and stay at the Greetham Valley.

The next day I carried on to Coltersworth via South and North Witham, to avoid the A1. Famous scientist Isaac Newton, he of apple on head and gravity fame, was born in nearby Woolsthorpe. In the church of St Mary's at North Witham it is alleged that there is graffiti scrawled by the young Newton, the scallywag. I can't say that I found any.

Luckily, at Coltersworth Ermine Street finally parted company with the A1 trunk road and I was able to get back on the straight and narrow to my next overnight stop, a pleasant B and B in Old Somerby. In the evening I had a tasty meal at the Fox and Hounds. Locals may have been wondering why a stranger bought a bottle of champagne to accompany his meal. Little did they realise that it was my way of celebrating the leaving behind of the A1 and A1M for good. From Little Stukeley to Coltersworth (almost 40 miles) the major artery had been built virtually on top of Ermine Street and I had been able to avoid travelling on it.

From Old Somerby, with a slight fuzziness in the head, due to all the bubbles in the champagne no doubt, I walked along a road called High Dyke. A dyke is an artificial embankment and this one was certainly raised. Margary (page 228) describes this section of road thus,

> "The Roman road is particularly impressive all along this stretch from Londonthorpe onwards, with a high-pitched agger, usually 3-4 feet and sometimes up to 6 feet high."

If you remember, an agger is the raised surface with ditches running alongside on which a Roman road is built. High Dyke is a long and very straight road without a footpath. However, I could see well ahead so was able to nip to one side of the road whenever the occasional lorry passed by. I made rapid progress and did the eight miles to Ancaster in under three hours. As suggested by the name, Ancaster is the site of a Roman fort and settlement. Just before reaching St Martin's church (named after a Roman soldier who converted to Christianity and eventually became bishop of Tours in France) I came across yet another apparently abandoned RAF airfield. However, to my surprise, it is still used; Barkston Heath, little changed since WWII, is used for elementary flying training and the planes are based at Cranwell. Perhaps the preponderance of old RAF stations has something to do with the extremely flat terrain of Cambridgeshire and Lincolnshire as well as the closeness of the European mainland.

Just over an hour later I arrived at Cranwell. During WWI airships used to operate out of the northern airfield here. Two roads in the village are named for this; the quirkily named Lighter Than Air Road and the boringly obvious Airship Road. I was unable to walk along either as entry was restricted to RAF personnel only. The main concrete runways are used by light aircraft. The equivalent of the army's Royal Military Academy Sandhurst, Royal Air Force College Cranwell is where all future officers in the RAF do their initial 24 weeks training. Two of the many notable graduates of Cranwell are Sir Frank Whittle, father of the jet propulsion engine, and Douglas Bader, the WWII flying ace who flew despite having two artificial legs. Whittle's ashes are interred in Cranwell.

At Cranwell, High Dyke crosses the A17. From here it runs as straight as a die to Waddington for another 12 miles, passing nothing but fields. Having already walked along its first 12 miles (Old Sowerby to Cranwell), I felt like a change so took the road that runs almost parallel to it, but at least passes through villages.

And so I ended up in Leadenham for the night in a B and B, as opposed to a C and C.

I set off in the morning along the ridgeline from Leadenham and ticked off two quaint villages in quick succession; Welbourn with the remains of a castle (well just a field really), and Wellingore (which used to have an RAF station, surprise, surprise). I then arrived at Navenby with the famous Mrs Smith's cottage museum. Who, I hear you ask? This native of Navenby died in 1995 aged 102. For most of her life she lived in a cottage that she bought in 1922 for £75. Fifteen years later electricity was installed. It was not until at least 1970 that she got an inside toilet and an inside cold water tap. These appear to be the only mod cons that she installed and they were put in to prevent the property being condemned as uninhabitable. On her death the cottage was bought by the local council and turned into a museum dedicated to the memory of Mrs Smith's simple way of life. It is funny how we see things differently as years go by. If Mrs Smith had been alive today, long before she reached old age, the council and aid agencies would have not allowed her to live the way she did. She would probably have been forced to leave her beloved cottage and go into sheltered housing. Sadly the cottage is now desperately in need of repair and not open to the public.

Just past Navenby is the amazingly named village of Boothby Grafoe. The remains (earthworks) of 13th century Somerton castle lie to the west of the village. And here's a nice link to earlier in my book – its layout was apparently very similar to that of Cooling castle in Kent (Jools Holland's home, remember?). Incidentally, a former Butlin's redcoat and comedian who was born in Hull has taken the name of the village as his stage name. Maybe I was expecting too much from a village with such a great name. In reality it is just a small village with a parish church that was rebuilt in 1666 after the original one was destroyed by a hurricane of all things.

Wandering into Coleby I was immediately struck by the height of the spire of All Saints; it seemed out of proportion to the rest of the church. I was also impressed by the vibrant colours of the hassocks (knee cushions) in the pews. They turned a fairly nondescript interior into a riot of colour. People had obviously enjoyed making these.

Carrying on towards Lincoln I reached Waddington, home to yet another RAF station. This one, however, actually does have aeroplanes flying in and out and I was buzzed continuously by a twin propeller craft practicing circuits. I don't think this is secret information, but here is the base of the RAF's main ISTAR airfield (Intelligence, Surveillance, Target Acquisition, and Reconnaissance). Interestingly, if you look at Google maps you can still see the faint outline of High Dyke (and thus Ermine Street) running through the south end of the runway.

And finally, at Bracebridge Heath, I got an unexpected and quite lovely view of the river Witham valley and Lincoln itself. I had been so used to the flat countryside that I had been walking through that I had quite forgotten that I had in fact been doing a ridge walk for many miles. I was surprised to find out that another thing on this ridge was the Viking Way, something that I had never heard of before. This is a long distance trail (147 miles) that runs from Humberside, via Lincoln, to Oakham. I must have criss-crossed this path on a number of occasions without realising it.

I was looking forward to seeing Lincoln in close up the next day. I had been there once before to visit one of my logistic depots. All I did on that occasion was drive to the city, park at the depot and drive out again without giving anywhere else a look. In those days I was unaware that this city was one of the major centres of Roman Britain. But first I needed to put my feet up. I had walked about 28 miles in two days and my back was telling me it needed a rest. City site-seeing with numerous coffee stops was called for.

But first a good night's sleep at the oddly named Tennyson hotel was in order. Why pick one of the nation's best known poets for the name of a hotel when Lincoln is bursting with history? All will be revealed.

11 LINCOLN (LINDUM)

Evidence of an Iron Age settlement in Lincoln was unearthed in 1972 near Brayford Pool. To the east of the Pool, typical Celtic wooden round houses and pottery, dating to around the 1st century BC, were excavated. Also, in 1826, on the west side of Lincoln in the river Witham, the Witham Shield was found. Dated to around 300BC, it is thought to have belonged to a local tribal chief. It is now housed in the British Museum. The name Lindon or Lindum probably gets the name from the Celtic word Lindo, meaning pool. Unfortunately, it has not been possible to determine the size of this community as later building by Romans, Normans and the modern city have long covered up any traces.

We do know with some certainty that the arrival of the Romans sparked a massive urban development. Lindsay Allason-Jones suggests in "Women in Roman Britain" (page 77) that,

> *"Sewerage systems have been uncovered in many Romano-British towns, and possibly the best were provided at Lincoln."*

Perhaps the building of these first class sewers was a portent of the importance that Lincoln would have as a strategic site, both during and long after the Roman occupation of Britain. The fact that Lincoln is sited on the top of a steep ridge at the confluence of the rivers Till and Witham would have made it a prime site for a major Roman fortress and town. The Witham makes its way eastwards to the Wash and North Sea, a ready supply route both for the garrison and for trading links as the town built up. The Till meanders northwest through prime agricultural land. In AD120 the Romans built a canal that linked Lincoln to the Trent, the third longest river in the United Kingdom. Using the fully navigable Trent, they had access to the fertile lands of the Midlands.

The strategic importance of the area can be inferred from the Roman road network around Lincoln. Ermine Street (Margary 2) passed through it and Fosse Way (Margary 5) terminated here, having started almost 250 miles away in Exeter. Another major Roman road (Margary 28) went to York via Doncaster. The Antonine Itinerary, a series of routes throughout the Roman Empire, created around the end of the second or start of the third century AD, identifies Lincoln as being on three of these routes. A map of those routes in Britain can be seen in M.C. Bishop's "The Secret History of the Roman Roads of Britain" (page 48).

The Ninth Legion had established a fortress here by around AD55, a short time before the Iceni revolt of AD60. Lands to the north were policed by the friendly Brigantes tribe under a client king relationship. In response to unrest within the Brigantine territory the Legion eventually moved north and established a base in York (AD71) and Lincoln became a colonia for retired soldiers. Peter Salway in "The Oxford Illustrated History of Roman Britain" (page 108) says,

> "The first [colonia for retired soldiers] *was founded at Lincoln, on the site of the disused legionary fortress. Its precise date is uncertain, though it is certainly Flavian and subsequent to the transfer away of its legion by 78 at the latest".

The previous model in Colchester whereby land was taken from the locals and given to the retired soldiers (and thus causing much disaffection) was not used in Lincoln. Salway says (page 110),

> "As a reserve of military strength and a centre of loyal influence, Colchester had been a failure, but this time the coloniae were not only tactfully situated, they were walled. The imperial government had learned its lesson".

The town soon grew beyond the limits of the fortress and eventually the original earth and wood construction was replaced by a stone defensive wall which also protected the civilian population of the rapidly expanded colonia.

During the fourth century, the conquered territory of Britain was split into four provinces to help tighten control; Britannia Prima's administrative headquarters was at Cirencester, Britannia Secunda's was York, Maxima Caesariensis had its capital in London, and Lincoln was the centre for Flavia Caesariensis.

Early in the fourth century, in AD306, Constantine was crowned emperor and shortly after he was converted to Christianity. Evidence of Christianity in Roman Britain is sparse. Although there must have been churches erected in the coloniae so far we only have one possible location; a small timber church underneath the site of St Paul in the Bail in Lincoln. Other tantalisingly small fragments also exist; pieces of lead pans used in the Cheshire salt mines contain inscriptions referring to a bishop Viventius and possible lead baptismal fonts with Christian symbols have been unearthed in eastern England. And, don't forget that I have also described previously about the hoard of Christian silverware that was found at Water Newton (chapter 10). Apart from these few historical fragments the evidence of Christianity in Roman Britain is so far non-existent.

As was typical in many of their urban and military centres, when the Romans left so did their trade. The town and waterways suffered through lack of interest and investment. However, perhaps because of its prime location, Lincoln eventually became a national focal point again, drawing Saxon, Viking and Norman invaders. Being only 130 easily accessible miles to London, the nation's capital, probably also added to Lincoln's appeal.

***

Vikings ruled Lincoln in the 9th and 10th centuries and the trading fortunes of the settlement rose again. Names like Bailgate, Danesgate, Skellingthorpe and Wragby are testimony to the presence of these Norsemen. In 1068 William the Conqueror led the Norman assault on the town and then ordered the building of both a castle and the cathedral. These were both situated in an area that once was within the original Roman fortress. By this time Christianity was the major religion in Western Europe. As befits the prowess of William, Lincoln Cathedral became the tallest building in the world in 1300 when the central tower was erected; the previous tallest man made structure having been the Great Pyramid in Egypt. Sadly the cathedral lost first place when a storm caused the spires to collapse in 1549. During this time Lincoln was the centre of the largest diocese in England, stretching from the Humber to the Thames.

Norman involvement in Lincoln was maintained well after William's death. Henry I died in 1135 with no male heir. His daughter, Matilda (also known as Maud for some reason) was the legitimate heir. However, Stephen of Blois, grandson of William I (the Conqueror) got a number of barons to support his claim and a civil war ensued. Lincoln Castle sided with Stephen. After the First Battle of Lincoln (1141) Stephen was captured. However, he eventually became king of England when a deal was struck with Matilda which ensured that her son would succeed Stephen. He became Henry II (he who had Thomas Becket murdered), the first Plantagenet king of England. If you recall, King Stephen was buried in the Abbey in Faversham and then his remains dug up and allegedly moved to an unmarked grave in the local church.

The next king to dally with Lincoln was John, the younger brother of Richard I. Whilst Richard was fighting in the Third Crusade, John sought to usurp the throne and in his support Lincoln Castle sided with him. This is where legend and fact become intertwined. That legendary hero of the people, Robin Hood, who robbed from the rich to give to the poor, supported King Richard and had many skirmishes against the Sheriff of Nottingham and Prince John. Robin and his band of merry men are famous for wearing Lincoln green outfits (apart from Will Scarlett who wore a red tunic). So much for the legend. The fact is that Lincoln became a very wealthy town based on its reputation for the weaving of fine cloth and woollen garments, dyed scarlet and green. Even modern day traffic wardens have bright green tops to their uniforms. The local football team, Lincoln City, has fallen in with the spirit of the colour scheme; they have gone for bright scarlet. Eventually John succeeded Richard and, falling foul of the barons, signed Magna Carta in 1215. One of the four remaining original copies of this document is housed in Lincoln Castle; this is probably because Hugh of Wells, Bishop of Lincoln, witnessed the signing of the document at Runnymede.

John, supported by the Pope, annulled Magna Carta which led to the Barons' War. His opponents persuaded Prince Louis of France to invade England to take the throne. Before a decisive confrontation with Louis and the barons John died. In 1216 his nine year old son became king, Henry III, ably supported by the regent William Marshall, Earl of Pembroke (probably one of the greatest statesmen this country has known). French troops led by the barons overran the town but the castle held out.

At the Second Battle of Lincoln in 1217 (76 years after the first battle), William Marshall defeated the French and they were eventually expelled from the country. Sadly, after the victory, looting of the town by William's troops took place. This event is euphemistically called "the Lincoln Fair". By this time Lincoln had become the third largest city in the country. Louis did not suffer too much from his failed dabble in British politics as he became Louis VIII, king of France.

Whilst being the centre of the largest Christian diocese, Lincoln was also home to one of the five most important Jewish communities in England. Sadly, as has been the lot of the Jews throughout the ages, they were persecuted here too. In 1190 anti-Semitic riots spread from King's Lynn in Norfolk. Sixty years later, there occurred the "Libel of Lincoln" in which 90 prominent Jews were wrongly accused of the ritual murder of a Christian boy, named Hugh. They were sent to the Tower of London and eventually 18 of their number were executed. Unfortunately, the anti-Semitism was fuelled by a Benedictine monk and chronicler, Matthew Paris. He wrote that Hugh was kidnapped, scourged, stabbed, crucified, disembowelled and thrown down a well. There was no evidence that any of this happened. Now here's another link to one of my earlier chapters; in the Prioress's Tale, one of Geoffrey Chaucer's Canterbury Tales, reference is made to Hugh of Lincoln. He was also known in medieval folklore as "Little Saint Hugh of Lincoln". The cathedral and town benefited for some time as many pilgrims were attracted to the place where "Saint Hugh" met his grizzly end. Henry III also benefited because the money and property of the 18 executed Jews became forfeit to the crown. By the end of the 13th century idiotic bigotry resulted in all Jews being expelled from Lincoln.

Lincoln then went into another period of economic decline. Boston, 35 miles southeast of Lincoln, lost its wool staple in 1353. This was a royal grant that allowed only certain ports to export wool. The effect of this was to reduce trade through Lincoln. During this period the castle became dilapidated. It was not until about 300 years later that Lincoln again became a key place. During the English Civil War control of the town seesawed between Cavaliers and Roundheads on numerous occasions. Finally in May 1645 the Parliamentarians stormed the castle and the town changed hands for the last time. The castle then became a regional jail until the last prisoners to be housed there left in 1878. It is still a crown court and has been since the 11th century.

During the Georgian era, Lincoln's fortunes were back on the up. The so called "British Agricultural Revolution", produced huge increases in farming efficiency in an area that was prime agricultural land. The reopening of the Foss Dyke canal (built by the Romans) meant that coal and other raw materials that fuelled industry could get to the city. The arrival of the railway also assisted the flow of materials in and out of Lincoln.

Another landmark, almost as prominent as the cathedral is the Westgate Water Tower. This giant tower, resembling a castle keep, was built as a result of a typhoid epidemic that hit Lincoln in 1904/5. Over 1,000 people were affected, of which more than a hundred died, including the man responsible for ensuring the town should have a good water supply. Polluted water from Hartsholme Lake and the river Witham was shown to be the cause. A new water source 20 miles away at Elkesley was identified and water was pumped from there to the tower. Maybe the 20th century townsfolk should have heeded the Romans. At Lincoln evidence has been unearthed that suggests that the Romans laid 20 miles of terracotta pipes to ensure a safe water supply.

Lincoln has had links with the military for a number of years. The first ever tanks were invented and built in the town by William Foster and Co during WWI. Sobraon barracks, home to part of the Logistics Corps, is named after a battle in 1846 between the East India Company and the Sikh Khalsa army. Incidentally, the East India Company (in a similar way to the impact of the siting of Roman forts on an area) is testimony to the power of trade in the development of towns and cities. Before the company arrived in

India and set up trading areas, the modern metropolises of Mumbai, Madras and Calcutta were tiny local communities.

***

With all of that history to look for I keenly set off on my day of sightseeing. I started my wander around Lincoln by looking for the point where Fosse Way and Ermine Street meet. I didn't have far to look as my hotel (The Tennyson) was within a few yards of this old junction. In the distance I could see the Cathedral about one mile straight ahead. Walking north along Ermine Street, the first historic building I came to was some way out from the city; St Mary's Guildhall, built in the 12th century. Due to it being outside of the old city limits I would assume that this building doesn't get a second glance as people rush to the centre. It is not until you walk over the railway level crossing, and the river Witham, that you start to almost fall over buildings from bygone times. Having said that, one's eye line is drawn inexorably towards the Cathedral so you could be forgiven for missing High Bridge and the river itself.

In comparison to the Ouse in York, Lincoln's river is a small, canal like channel. The barges I saw did not seem out of place. However, as mentioned previously, it was deep enough for navigation and providing trading links to the North Sea.

From High Bridge, the straight line of Ermine Street continues under the archway of Lincoln Guildhall. The arch is called Stonebow. The Guildhall dates to around 1520 and has been the meeting place for the city council since medieval times. Having already mentioned about Lincoln's ignominious past with regards to the treatment of the Jews, I then noted that Ermine Street goes past the building called the Jew's House (now a restaurant). The Jew's House was at the centre of the once thriving Jewish population of Lincoln. Built in the 12th century, some of the original features still survive (the arched doorway and windows and stonework on the upper floor).

From the Jews House, Ermine Street goes up Steep Hill and true to its name, it was steep; and having walked up it I can confirm that it is a lot steeper than it looks.

Margary describes it succinctly (page 229),

"The road [Ermine Street] *continued straight up the old street called (rightly) Steep Hill to the centre of Roman Lincoln (Lindum Colonia). This road must be the most striking example of the Roman indifference to steep gradients, at least in the layout of their primary roads, for the hill is entirely useless to all modern traffic except on foot."*

Before popping into the Cathedral I visited the tourist information centre, not seeking to find any information, but simply because it is such an attractive building. It was formerly Leigh-Pemberton House, one of Lincoln's oldest. Built in 1543 for a merchant, it later became a bank before being given to the city in the latter half of the 20th century. Apparently the upper floors are self-catering apartments.

Once I arrived at the Cathedral I found it so big that, no matter where I stood to take a photograph, I could not do it justice.

Outside on the west front there was a spider's web of scaffolding. A successful bid to The Heritage Lottery Fund has ensured that much needed renovation to the 12th century Romanesque frieze of this Norman building can take place. The building work is expected to take until 2023 to be completed. Once inside it felt very impersonal, even though there was a service going on. In comparison, Canterbury and Chelmsford cathedrals had felt quite inviting. The cathedral would have a different feel soon after my visit, however. Lincolnshire has long associations with the Royal Air Force and on leaving Lincoln I would be visiting RAF Scampton. It was pleasing to find out that the cathedral will be hosting a memorial dinner to celebrate 100 years of the RAF in August 2018.

Next to the cathedral is the Priory Arch. This is a Victorian replacement of an original medieval entrance to the cathedral close. Close by was a statue honouring the poet Sir Alfred Lord Tennyson, a native of Lincolnshire. Ah, I now understand why my hotel in Lincoln was called the Tennyson. I then saw the remains of the Lincoln Medieval Bishop's Palace which used to be the administrative centre of the largest diocese in medieval England, stretching from the Humber to the Thames. It even has a mini vineyard.

My time was slipping away and energy levels were quickly running low so I swiftly walked westwards to the Castle and its copy of Magna Carta.

Earlier in this chapter I described the role that the castle had played in a number of key events in English history so it was rather nice to wander around the ancient building. York may have far more historical places to see but at least the castle is still standing in Lincoln.

From the castle there were two more places I definitely wanted to see, part of the Roman ruins of the city. The first, the Newport Roman Arch was Ermine Street's way north out of the city. This is still used as a route for modern traffic. The second was in the grounds of the Lincoln hotel; part of the Roman wall. I am rather embarrassed to say that by the time I got to these parts of the city my camera battery life died on me so I was unable to take pictures of the two Roman ruins. On the internet I found a cracking black and white picture of an old lorry's altercation with the Newport Arch.

At the end of the day, like my camera, my internal battery was on empty and, with a sense of monument fatigue, I was longing to recharge and hit the open road. You can have too much of a good thing after all.

12 LINCOLN TO THE HUMBER

Route: Margary 2d (pages 236-238).

My route out of Lincoln was in a northerly direction following Ermine Street. I say this because there was an alternative Roman way to York. Margary (page 190) says,

> "Lincoln was an important place, and from it several roads diverged. Ermine Street continued its northward course to the Humber in a most impressively undeviating fashion, and at a point a few miles from Lincoln a branch led off north-westward, crossing the river Trent at Littleborough, to give another route to York, through Doncaster, that would avoid the Humber crossing."

In the morning I left Lincoln with great enthusiasm. I was walking a section of Ermine Street that is described in glowing terms by Margary. On page 236 he states that,

> "When everything is considered, this section of Ermine Street must be one of the most magnificent in the whole of Britain … it still remains a thoroughfare almost throughout its 32 miles, much of it a fine main road which yet maintains its highly raised appearance and Roman character to a quite remarkable degree."

All I can say is that Margary did not try walking along this "magnificent" stretch of Ermine Street in the 21st century. Yes, it is long, straight and raised and may have oodles of Roman character for all I know. However, it is also the A15, a major trunk road linking Lincolnshire with the Humber Bridge. I walked as far as the junction of the A15 and A46, got fed up with the traffic, turned back to the city, went west along Queen Elizabeth Road for half a mile and came to the B1398 and turned back north towards Burton. This road and Middle Street combine to follow in a northerly direction not far from Ermine Street. My research found out that these roads follow the path of an ancient trackway, so I was rather pleased that I would be walking this route. Also, as I was hiking along another long wide ridge line (which Ermine Street followed too) it was easy to forget that on either side the land is extremely flat for as far as the eye could see.

Quickly walking through three small villages, Burton, South and North Carlton (each with their own church, of course), I arrived at Scampton. On the face of it, this is an unremarkable hamlet, just like many others in the area. However, the name of the village pub and its sign give away the importance in the nation's psyche; the pub sign has a Lancaster bomber on it. The hostelry is called the Dam Busters Arms. Almost within a stone's throw is the southern end of a runway, the northern end of which cuts across Ermine Street. It was way too early for lunch at the pub so I wandered over to RAF Scampton and the Heritage Centre. Whilst chatting with the person on guard duty he asked me where I was aiming for. When I said that I was looking to get to where Ermine Street meets the Humber at Winteringham, he amazed me by saying that that was where he comes from. As I have said previously, it's a small world. I spent a very leisurely two hours looking at the exhibits. The Red Arrows aeronautical display team are based at Scampton so there were various items relating to that.

Also, I was interested to read about the Vulcan bombers which were based here. This delta wing aircraft was a design of beauty, an odd thing to say when one considers its purpose; they were part of our nuclear deterrent. I remember seeing a Vulcan at the Woodford air show in Cheshire when I was a teenager. The noise of the aircraft as it took off was the loudest thing I had ever come across. Goodness knows what the villagers of Scampton thought, especially as they knew that the Vulcans were carrying nuclear weapons.

Strangely enough, the most moving thing I saw was Nigger's grave. According to the 1955 film, The Dam Busters, Nigger was wing commander Guy Gibson's black Labrador which got run over on the day of the raid on German dams during WWII. I had always thought that this was a bit of dramatic licence until I saw the inscription on the dog's grave.

> *"Nigger was killed by a car on 16th May 1943. Buried at midnight as his owner was leading his squadron on the attack against the Mohne and Eder dams."*

The highly decorated Gibson (Victoria Cross etc.) survived the raid, codenamed Operation Chastise, but later died in action in September 1944 aged only 26. Back outside the gates at the RAF base I looked back south along Ermine Street towards Lincoln. It was five miles yet I could still see the cathedral standing proudly on the ridge line. I walked back to the Dam Busters pub for lunch and whilst looking at the memorabilia could not help but reflect on the immense bravery that some people are capable of. I then had a peaceful stroll to my overnight stop, a small b and b in Glentworth.

The following day I made steady, if nondescript, progress through the Lincolnshire countryside, passing through numerous villages along the way. I made a right turn at Greetwell (saw no-one to greet there) crossed over the A15 and ended up at Scawby for the night at another b and b. Whilst on the bridge I noticed that the A15 below was extremely busy (plenty of articulated lorries) and had no pedestrian footpath, so I was pleased that I had chosen to walk for two days along the route of the ancient trackway from Lincoln.

In Scawby I popped into the parish church for no other reason than it had what I thought was an unusual name, St Hybald.

In his Ecclesiastical History, St Bede describes Hybald as "a most holy and continent man". Now, I assumed that an incontinent man would be one who could not wait to go to the toilet. So, would a continent man be able to hold things in until he arrives at a lavatory? Not believing an ability to do that would warrant someone being made a saint, I looked up in the dictionary what incontinent means. In addition to loose bowels, it also refers to someone who cannot say no regarding controlling temper and sexual urges. The church should have been closed but luckily a young man was busy dusting the pews and so I was able to pop inside. He was very proud of his church and I was pleased when he stopped the dusting and talked about it to me. He dug out a folder of old photographs dating to as far back as the early 20th century and I spent a leisurely half hour thumbing through it.

The next morning I made my way north for two miles to Broughton and was then back on the line of Ermine Street; the A15 having stopped at its junction with the M180. A ten minute walk from Broughton is Wressle. You may find this hard to believe but a monumental tussle in Wressle had taken place with regards to drilling for oil. Well, maybe I am exaggerating slightly. In June 2013 a company got temporary planning permission to drill a conventional oil well on farmland. This wasn't the contentious fracking but a bog standard well that you may have seen on Dallas, the famous TV series about feuding oil families. Following the test drilling in 2015, analysis estimated that the site could produce 710 barrels of oil per day. Planning permission was applied for to develop the site. After two years of appeals this permission had still not been granted.

Carrying on northwards I came to Winterton, on the west side of which lies Old Cliff Farm, site of a Roman villa. There is evidence in the area of a number of old building complexes that may have been villas too. The neighbouring village of Winteringham used to be a crossing point for the ferry across the Humber. Interestingly, the Romans did not fortify Ermine Street from Lincoln to the Humber, apart from building a fort at Winteringham. Their main line of forts linking with York followed a gentle curve around the Humber. They did, however, build forts on the north side between Brough and York and I would be following this part of Ermine Street in the next chapter.

Having reached Winteringham, I could almost see my hotel in Brough, three miles across the Humber as the crow flies. As I am not a crow a thought struck me, "How the hell do I get there?" It would take me a ridiculously circuitous route of 15 miles via the Humber Bridge, that's how. At this bleak and lonely spot where Ermine Street meets the Humber someone had kindly erected an information board that celebrated the Roman connection (see below).

I could see the Humber Bridge, about eight miles to the east. Margary's book had suggested that Lincoln to Brough is 32 miles. I had done that just getting to Winteringham. On the basis that I had walked the required distance, I used public transport to cover the detour (the number 350 from Winteringham to Hessle and then the number 155 to Brough). The truly magnificent bridge, a grade 1 listed building, was opened to traffic in 1981 and it has an expected shelf life of around 120 years. It is the longest single span suspension bridge in the world that pedestrians can walk across; the central span is 1.4 km (0.88 miles). It costs a very reasonable £1.50 for cars to use. Using my bus pass it cost me nothing. Having traversed the Humber I got a sense that I was finally back up north, back in God's own country.

***

Following a night's rest in Brough, from the Humber to York was not expected to take me more than three days, including a detour to Stamford Bridge. It took the Romans slightly longer. The colonisation of Britannia beyond the Humber to York and Hadrian's Wall was not completed until thirty years after the initial invasion. The progress of the Roman legions north and west did not make headway as rapidly as their initial advance on Colchester (completed within the first campaign season of the invasion). Supply lines had to be formed and protected as well as hostile bands of warriors subdued. As these supply lines extended so the movement of troops and goods took longer. Other unforeseen events would also have slowed down the rate of conquest. Prior to advancing beyond the Humber, one such episode took place in AD60-61. Despite it lasting a mere few months out of the millennia of British history, it seems to have maintained a hold on the national psyche far greater than the importance of the occasion itself. Even a statue was erected on Victoria Embankment, near Westminster Bridge in London, in 1850 to commemorate the event. I am talking about the Boudiccan revolt. By the way, the Britons did not put scythes on their war chariots as indicated in the sculpture. They would have ripped the horses' legs to shreds on other chariots.

The Iceni tribe were based in the area covered by Norfolk and Suffolk. Their king, Prasutagus, had seen the advantage of forming a treaty with the Romans rather than do battle with them. He became a client king. To pay for local and provincial Roman government, and maintenance of the Imperial army and its pensioners, taxes were levied and accepted, albeit reluctantly, by the indigenous population. Such was the price of a peace treaty. To raise revenue, these taxes could take numerous forms; individual poll tax per head of population, toll based on use of routes and harbours, land tax based on size and amount produced on the land (including minerals as well as food). When administered fairly these taxes were seen as an unavoidable way of life, the price of peace. Unfortunately, this fairness was missing.

Patricia Southern in "Roman Britain a New History 55BC-AD450" (page 107) says,

> "In this climate of Roman taxation and corrupt administration, it is not surprising that Prasutagus, the ruler of the Iceni, had made provision in his will for sharing his kingdom between his family and the Roman Emperor, hoping to protect his people from the greed of the provincial officials."

Following the death of Prasutagus, avaricious officials wanted it all. Southern goes on to say (page 107),

> "The official in charge of financial affairs, the procurator Decianus Catus, descended on the Iceni, backed up by a few Roman troops, to claim the inheritance for Nero."

Adding to this fiscal corruption, Lindsay Allason-Jones in "Women in Roman Britain" (page 56) says that,

> "There is evidence of land grants to some veterans at Colchester, Lincoln and Gloucester in the first century, as the State tried to establish official settlements, but this was rarely successful – the boorish behaviour of the veterans at Colchester, for example, was a contributory factor to the dissatisfaction which led to the Boudiccan revolt."

The Romans called those people that they had conquered peregrini. As this means foreigners that must have really upset the Britons. For seventeen years since the invasion the tribes had been under military rule. This rule had involved exploitation and abuse. Patricia Southern sums up conditions well (page 94),

> "They lived where the Romans said they should live, obeying new rules, and they would keep the peace with each other, or else! For most of the Britons, who were not among the

favoured elite, this so-called Pax Romana just after the conquest did not bring peace and prosperity."

A spark could ignite the simmering rage that was felt by the subjugated. When it came, that spark was a flame. It is not known why, but following a protest from Prasutagus's wife, Boudicca, she was flogged and her daughters raped. Tacitus in "The Annals" (page 319) says,

> *"Right at the start Prasutagus's wife Boudicca was flogged and his daughters raped. All the leading Iceni were divested of their ancestral property, as though the Romans had been made a gift of the whole region, and the king's relatives were dealt with as slaves."*

Whereas people's hero, Robin Hood, was a folk legend, Boudicca was a real person with legendary status. Perhaps we can blame Cassius Dio for this. In "Roman History, Books 61-70" (pages 85-105) he describes her in almost hero-worship detail and quotes her rousing call to arms speech as if he were present amongst the listening Iceni. On page 85 Dio says,

> *"But the person who was chiefly instrumental in rousing the natives and persuading them to fight the Romans … was Buduica* [yet another spelling of the name], *a Briton woman of the royal family and possessed of greater intelligence than often belongs to women. This woman assembled her army, to the number of some 120,000 … In stature she was very tall, in appearance most terrifying, in the glance of her eye most fierce, and her voice was harsh; a great mass of the tawniest hair fell to her hips; around her neck was a large golden necklace; and she wore a tunic of divers colours over which a thick mantle was fastened with a brooch. This was her invariable attire. She now grasped a spear to aid her in terrifying all beholders and spoke as follows: … "*

In a speech that stands alongside the one that Queen Elizabeth I made to her troops during the Spanish Armada threat, Dio "quotes" Boudicca (pages 89-91),

> *"… Have no fear whatever of the Romans; for they are superior to us neither in numbers nor in bravery … Indeed, we enjoy such a surplus of bravery, that we regard our tents as safer than their walls and our shields as affording greater protection than their whole suits of mail … But these are not the only respects in which they are vastly inferior to us: there is also the fact that they cannot bear up under hunger, thirst, cold, or heat, as we can … Furthermore, this region is familiar to us and is our ally, but to them it is unknown and hostile. As for rivers, we swim them naked, whereas they do not get across them easily even in boats … Let us show them that they are hares and foxes trying to rule over dogs and wolves."*

Great stuff; the sort of language that would enthral Cassius Dio's audiences and readers back in Rome.

The Iceni took up arms (along with some other tribes, including the Trinovantes). Romanised towns were attacked (Colchester, London and St Albans), destroyed and their populations slaughtered. These would have been seen as easy targets. Tacitus (page 319) says,

> *"And wiping out a colony surrounded by no fortifications did not seem a difficult undertaking – our commanders, paying more attention to aesthetics than utility, had taken too little precaution in this regard."*

It would seem that the sequence of events according to Tacitus (pages 320-321) was:

1. Camulodunum destroyed: *"Everything else was pillaged or burned by their onset, but the temple in which the soldiers*

had gathered was subjected to a two-day blockade and then taken by storm."

2. Ninth Legion overwhelmed: *"Moreover, the triumphant Britons met Petillius Cerialis, legate of the Ninth Legion* [which was based in Lincoln], *who was coming to relieve the Romans, and they put his legion to flight and killed all his infantry. Cerialis escaped to his camp with the cavalry and found protection within his fortifications."*

3. Londinium sacked: *"While it did not have the distinction of being designated a 'colony', the town was nevertheless famed for its large concentration of businessmen and saleable goods. There Seutonius vacillated over whether he should choose it as his base of operations; but when he considered his small numbers, and the clear evidence of the severe penalty Petillius had paid for headstrong action, he decided on saving the overall situation by the sacrifice of a single town ... All who were held back because their sex disqualified them from fighting, or because they were feeble with age or had attachments to the locality, were overwhelmed by the enemy."*

4. Verulamium (St Albans) looted: *"The same disaster befell the town of Verulamium, because the barbarians, who revelled in plunder and were averse to hard work, bypassed strongholds and garrisoned positions to make for the military granary – rich pickings for a looter and difficult for its defenders to secure."*

Treatment by the Britons of some women was a chilling forerunner of punishments handed out at the end of the Second World War to those women who fraternised with German occupation forces. British females who married Romans were seen as traitors. According to Cassius Dio, page 95,

"Those who were taken captive by the Britons were subjected to every known form of outrage. The worst and most bestial atrocity committed by their captors was the following. They hung up naked the noblest and most distinguished women and then cut off their breasts and sewed them to their mouths, in order to make the victims appear to be eating them; afterwards they impaled the women on sharp skewers run lengthwise through the entire body."

Tacitus adds (page 321),

"It is well established that some 70,000 Roman citizens and allies lost their lives in the locations I have mentioned. For the Britons did not take captives, or sell them, or indulge in any other wartime trafficking, rather, they hastily resorted to slaughter, the gallows, burning, and crucifixion, accepting that they would face punishment, but meanwhile take revenge for it ahead of time."

There were some sites which would have been singled out as prime targets. Patricia Southern (page 84) says that,

"The establishment of the Imperial Cult in Colchester, no matter to whom the temple was dedicated, would have been particularly galling for the Britons, especially for those wo had submitted voluntarily and then found out that the Roman peace actually entailed exploitation and abuse. Those men who participated in the cult would probably have been immediate targets for the rebels under Boudicca."

The temple in Colchester was also seen as a red rag to a bull by Tacitus (page 319),

"Furthermore, a temple erected to the deified Claudius lay before the natives' eyes like a bastion of everlasting domination, and the men chosen as its priests were pouring away whole fortunes in the name of religion."

Suetonius Paulinus, who was appointed governor of Britain in AD58, was campaigning in North Wales at the time of the revolt. He led his XIV Legion back along Watling Street and faced Boudicca's army in an unknown location. Towcester and High Cross have been suggested as possible battle sites. In the explanatory notes in Tacitus (page 487) it says,

> "The site of Boudicca's last battle has been subject of much antiquarian debate, with rival locations ranging from the outskirts of Prestatyn to King's Cross Station (platform 9). The most likely spot is near Mancetter, on Watling Street in the Midlands."

The Roman army of 10,000 men faced a massive force. Cassius Dio takes up the story (page 97),

> "Buduica, at the head of an army of about 230,000 men, rode in a chariot herself ... Paulinus could not extend his line the whole length of hers, for even if the men had been drawn up only one deep, they would not have reached far enough, so inferior were they in numbers; nor, on the other and, did he dare join battle in a single compact force, for fear of being surrounded and cut to pieces. He therefore separated his army into three divisions, in order to fight at several points at one and the same time, and he made each of the divisions so strong that it could not easily be broken through."

Dio says that Paulinus then roused each division with separate speeches (reminiscent of Henry V at Agincourt). The battle raged all day and Dio concludes the event (pages 103-105),

> "But finally, late in the day, the Romans prevailed; and they slew many in battle beside the wagons and the forest, and captured many alive. Nevertheless, not a few made their escape and were preparing to fight again. In the meantime, however, Buduica fell sick and died. The Britons mourned her

deeply and gave her a costly burial; but feeling that now at last they were really defeated, they scattered to their homes. So much for affairs in Britain."

According to Tacitus (page 322),

"The glory won that day was spectacular, equal to that of victories of old, for some reports put the British dead at not much below 80,000 with roughly 400 Roman soldiers killed and not many more wounded. Boudicca ended her life with poison."

Don't forget that Tacitus, like Cassius Dio, was reporting well after the event and to an audience of Romans. Whatever the true figures, it was an overwhelming Roman victory. At first, Suetonius Paulinus conducted a vicious campaign of retribution. However, in an attempt at reconciliation in the name of the future peace of the province, he was replaced by Petronius, a more benign governor.

And what happened to Boudicca after she poisoned herself? Local legend says that she is buried beneath track ten at King's Cross Station in London.

13 BROUGH ON HUMBER TO YORK

Route: Margary 2e (pages 418-419).

Brough on Humber (Petuaria Parisiorum, named after the Celtic Parisi tribe from the area) was the third civitas that I visited (Canterbury and Water Newton being the other two). It is the smallest of the Roman towns listed by David Mattingly in "An Imperial Possession, Britain in the Roman Empire" (pages 328-329), being only 6 hectares in area, compared to Canterbury at 52 hectares and Water Newton at 18 hectares. During the 2nd century an earthwork defence was erected. In later centuries a wall and bastion towers were added. It is believed to have been one of the centres of the mosaic industry. Peter Salway in "The Oxford Illustrated History of Roman Britain" (page 459) says,

> "Another trade centred on certain Romano-British towns, but carrying out much of its actual work in the villas, was the mosaic industry. It can be fairly described as industrial, because it is clear that there were at least four, possibly five, identifiable schools of mosaicists – whether large firms or groups of craftsmen working in a common style and using common pattern-books we do not know – centred on Cirencester, Chesterton (Water Newton), Dorcester (Dorset), Brough-on-Humber, and somewhere in the centre of the south."

I suppose that when thinking of the Romans, at some point people think of their legacy of villas and mosaic floors and walls. Salway mentions (page 461),

"All [the mosaic schools] *were at their peak in the fourth century, laying pavements chiefly in villas, and clearly responding to the flowering of villa life in the first half of the century."*

That villa life flowered in the early fourth century may be down to the fact that prominent Romans moved from their primary abodes on the continent to Britain following unrest and Germanic incursions in AD276; well to do Roman citizens were seeking to protect their capital. Salway says (page 193),

"Fifty to sixty towns are reported to have been captured by the barbarians and subsequently recovered by the Romans. Archaeology shows large numbers of villas in northern Gaul as apparently abandoned from the late third century. In consequence, it has been suggested that the remarkable flowering of villas in Britain from 270 onwards reflects a 'flight of capital' from Gaul."

It seems that the concept of finding a place in the country, as championed on daytime TV programmes, is nothing new.

There must have been a ferry across the Humber at this point as Ermine Street carries on from Lincoln to York here. Despite its lack of size, I was hoping to find some recognition of a Roman past. Sadly, I found nothing, save one street name (Centurion Way) that hinted at the town's imperial past. At least in Water Newton you could see faint outlines of former buildings in a field. Neither did I find reference to highwayman Dick Turpin; apparently he lived in Brough before being executed for horse theft. Soon all traces of the town's aeronautical past will disappear too. BAE built the Hawk jet trainer here and used the adjoining runway. With over 800 redundancies having occurred, the airfield is steadily being built over.

That there actually was a Roman town in Brough is certain. Lindsay Allason-Jones in "Women in Britain" (page 164) says,

"... there is an inscription referring to a theatre in Petuaria although the actual structure has yet to be found."

Patricia Southern elaborates in "Roman Britain a New History, 55BC – AD450" (page 180),

"Only very rarely is there any indication of who built these splendid new amenities, but at Brough-on-Humber an inscription states that Marcus Ulpius Januarius, an aedile of the town, built a theatre. This is the only inscription mentioning an aedile in Britain."

However, this may not have been a permanent structure. So, we have evidence of the inscription but not the theatre. Incidentally, an aedile was a civil servant who supervised the maintenance of public buildings and occasionally public order.

Although any evidence of the Roman ferry crossing is long gone, the names of nearby towns on either side of the Humber hint at this (South and North Ferriby). I love the next bit. In 1931 a local man found two planks of wood at the edge of the Humber. Now I would have assumed that they were any old fragments of wood from a boat. These were in fact the only evidence outside Egypt of sewn plank boats. These bits of flotsam were Bronze Age items dating to before 1600BC.

You can imagine the conversation:

"Here, Doris come and look at these Bronze Age treasures I have just found by the river."

"Come off it, Sid. You've had a bit too much sun. Make yourself useful and go into the shed and make a seesaw for the kids out of them."

From Brough I walked to South Cave. Confusingly, the name has nothing to do with a cave. Apparently, the word cave comes from caf, meaning swift. Just before entering the village of South Newbald the original Roman road forked; my route going northwest and the northeast one eventually reaching the important Roman fort and settlement at Malton. A few hundred yards further on I came to North Newbald and had to be on my best behaviour. It was here that the last public flogging in Britain is alleged to have taken place. There is supposed to be a whipping post on the pretty village green. I only found a phone box and letter box.

The next small town I arrived at, Market Weighton, has a geological feature named after it, the Market Weighton Axis. It is on the line of tectonic plate movements that took place during the Triassic period. The area may have felt the earth move too when William Bradley walked through the streets. This local celebrity (died in 1820 aged 33) was 7ft 9inches tall and weighed in at 27 stones. A wooden statue was erected in honour of him being the tallest man in Britain (see below). Even in the late 20th century they celebrated his memory with the Giant Bradley Festival. When I showed his photograph to my Mum, she asked if his height included the plinth – bless her.

Another person from Market Weighton who helped the earth move, but in a political manner, was Barbara Foxley who died aged 98 in 1958. She was the daughter of the local vicar and moved to Cardiff University to take up a teaching post. She was a fervent activist in the cause of female rights and in 1918 became a member of the executive committee of the National Union of Societies for Equal Citizenship.

Having spent a night at a local B and B I made my way to Pocklington. Twenty years after William the Conqueror's invasion this, now small town, was in fact the second biggest in what would become Yorkshire, with York being the largest. The town grew as a result of it being the centre of the English woollen trade; wool being England's main export to the rest of Europe during the Middle Ages (5th to 15th centuries). Some of the inhabitants of Pocklington may have been woolly minded too. The "Flying Man of Pocklington", Thomas Pelling, made a set of wings and tried to fly from the church roof. Sadly, and inevitably, he died in the attempt. Whereas most people would have drawn a veil over this, the townsfolk of Pocklington run a Flying Man festival in his honour. Another idiosyncratic, and dare I say, typically loopy, English event is the Pocktoberfest; this being Pocklington's answer to Munich's Oktoberfest. Whereas the latter is a celebration of Bavarian beer, food and entertainment, it would appear that the English version skips the food and entertainment and focuses on just the beer. I am so proud to be English knowing that Pocklington and many other places around the country preserve the essential art of not taking oneself too seriously. Pocklington is also home to the more sober pastime of gliding.

And then I arrived at Wilberfoss, the village that was home to many generations of the Wilberforce family. One member of the family, who lived in nearby Hull, was William Wilberforce. He became an independent member of parliament for Yorkshire and a lifelong anti-slavery campaigner. It is shocking to realise that only four years before Victoria became queen, it was still seen as legally acceptable for one man to own another; this from a country that regarded itself as Christian in outlook and behaviour. Whilst remembered as a one cause politician, Wilberforce was a complex character who was castigated for not supporting enough the improvement in working conditions in England whilst championing the conditions of slaves abroad. He wanted habeas corpus suspended and opposed the inquiry into the Peterloo Massacre where 11 people were killed at a rally organised to demand political reform. He opposed organisations that supported workers' rights. On the other hand, he did support the improvement in conditions for chimney sweeps and textile workers and was interested in prison reform and the Society for the Prevention of Cruelty to Animals. Three days before William Wilberforce died in 1833, the Slavery Abolition Act was passed.

***

Having rested overnight in Wilberfoss, I made what I thought was my longest and final detour off the straight and narrow and ended up at Stamford Bridge. Whereas Margary's route does not go via Stamford Bridge, research undertaken by the Roman Roads Research Association suggests that Ermine Street does in fact go through the town. So, I wasn't taking a detour after all; I was in fact on the right track. This village lies a few miles east of the city of York and is the site of an old crossing point of the river Derwent. I wanted to visit the site of one of the pivotal battles in British history. In typical English understatement, there is a block of rock on Main Street (and another equally low key lump of stone in Whiterose Drive) that commemorates this critical battle.

On 5th January 1066, Edward the Confessor died childless. There were four potential candidates as his successor. In order of strength of claim, strongest first, they were:

Edgar the Aetheling (means belonging to a noble family) probably had the only truly legitimate claim to the throne. He was of solid Saxon stock and could trace his roots back to Alfred the Great. His father had been removed from the throne by Cnut the Dane, who made himself king. Unfortunately, Edgar was a boy at the time that the Saxons were looking for a strong leader to help defend the realm against the Vikings and Normans. As a result the true heir got little or no backing from the country's nobles.

Harold Hardrada, king of Norway, claimed the throne through being a distant relative of Cnut, king of England, Norway and Denmark. Cnut's son Hardicanute, became king following Cnut's death. In turn, Hardicanute promised the throne to Magnus, Harold Hardrada's father. Before Magnus could become king, Edward the confessor took the crown.

Harold Godwinson became related to Edward the Confessor when Edward married Harold's sister. So he had no blood link. He was the Saxon earl of Wessex and one of the richest men in the country. Being a good leader and strong warrior, the English nobles saw the attributes they were looking for that they did not see in Edgar the Aetheling.

William of Normandy had the weakest claim. He was a distant cousin of Edward the Confessor. William claimed that Edward had promised him the throne twenty years before he died. In addition Harold Godwinson who had been shipwrecked in Normandy was alleged to have sworn to support William's claim.

Incidentally, Cnut, or Canute as he is often called, has gone down in history as the nutter (should that be cnutter?) who unsuccessfully commanded the tide not to come in. He was in fact one of the nation's greatest kings who was merely trying to demonstrate to sycophantic followers that he was not a god but a mere mortal.

On his deathbed, Edward named Harold Godwinson as his heir. The Witan, the king's council, unanimously confirmed this decision. So Harold became king. With all the claims and counter claims he knew that he would have to fight to maintain his crown. He assumed the main threat would come from Normandy, perhaps because he remembered offering allegiance to William. Also, William had got the moral support of the Pope who believed that Harold had broken his promise. If all of the above was not confusing enough, Harold's brother, Tostig Godwinson, allied himself to Harold Hardrada and between them they planned an invasion in the north.

During the summer of 1066 king Harold waited in the south of England anticipating a Norman invasion. The army led by Hardrada and Tostig struck first. At the battle of Fulford on 20th September 1066 they defeated the local Saxon forces and York capitulated. The victorious army based itself at Stamford Bridge, awaiting supplies. Expecting King Harold to stay down south to fend off William, many of their troops were allowed to go back to the beachhead at Ricall on the banks of the river Ouse. However, on hearing of the invasion in the north King Harold marched his men to Tadcaster, eight miles from York. They covered the 185 miles in six days. The Norwegians were not aware that Harold had arrived. On 25th September the Saxon army advanced to York and then Stamford Bridge.

The Saxons numbered around 10,000 with estimates of the Norwegian army being half that. It is thought that at least 3,000 had gone back to the beachhead. The king's men took the invaders by surprise. Despite rallying his troops, Harold Hardrada was killed early in the battle. The king offered his brother Tostig an amnesty which was refused. Eventually Tostig and most of his men were killed. The Norwegian reinforcements from the beachhead arrived too late to make a difference. In defeat they fought fiercely and many Saxon warriors were killed, among them the elite houscarls. Harold Godwinson had been victorious but at a great cost to his numbers and experience.

There was no time to celebrate this hard won victory as Harold learnt that William had landed and established fortresses at Pevensey and Hastings. Harold would have used Ermine Street in his rapid march south to meet William the Conqueror's forces. On 14th October, at the Battle of Hastings, Harold and many of his Saxon troops were killed and the reign of the Normans began. Had Harold been defeated by the Vikings then William would have been able to march unimpeded on London. With a Viking victory in the north perhaps they could have expanded their army with Saxon warriors opposed to the Normans which may have been capable of defeating William's army.

It is amazing that the future of a nation hinged on the outcomes of two battles (Stamford Bridge and Hastings), and that each lasted less than a day but had implications that endured for hundreds of years and influenced world history. When I was in the Air Training Corps we used to discuss the "what if" implications of not winning the Battle of Britain in WW2. If Harold had lost at Stamford Bridge perhaps there would not have been a Battle of Britain.

One thing that had always puzzled me was why is Chelsea football club's ground called Stamford Bridge? When I was younger I assumed that this was the site of the old battle between the Saxons and Vikings. How naïve. Apparently, it gets the name from Samfordesbrigge, which means the bridge at the sandy ford. Whilst on the subject of football (not quite as boring as formula one racing which is the second most boring sport in the world) why is one of Liverpool's stands called the Kop? This originates from the battle of Spion Kop near Ladysmith during the second Boer War in South Africa. In 1904 at Arsenal's ground, a reporter thought that the steep football terrace reminded him of the soldiers standing on the hill during the battle. In 1906 a reporter made a similar observation about Liverpool's new stand. And getting back nicely to Roman roads, Leicester City has a Kop stand called the Fosse Stand. But that is another Roman road altogether.

And the most boring sport in the world, I hear you ask? Well, there has to be a sport more boring that formula one racing but I have not yet come across it. I popped onto a less frenetic motor vehicle, the number 10 bus from Stamford Bridge and covered the ten miles to York in around 40 minutes. At a speed of 180 miles per hour a formula one car could have reached my house 120 miles away in that time. With that utterly useless snippet racing through my mind I made my way towards my hotel in York.

***

As I approached York I gave myself a pat on the back. I had followed in the footsteps of the Ninth Legion all the way from Richborough in Kent, having set off on my adventure from Penrith in Cumbria. But where had the Legion commenced its journey? To be more precise, what had the Ninth Legion been up to prior to its arrival in Britain and where did it end up? It was formed by Pompey in 65BC and then took part in all conflicts in the Roman Republic era up to the formation of the Empire in 27BC. Prior to becoming the first Roman emperor, Augustus used the Ninth Legion in his fight against Mark Antony. It then went to the Iberian Peninsula where it gained the title "Legio Hispania", army of Spain. Here it took part in Augustus's campaigns against the Cantabrians until 13BC.

In AD14 Tiberius became the second emperor, following the suspicious death of his step father Augustus. For a short while there was a risk of mutiny by a number of legions. The Ninth was based in Pannonia in the northeast of the Empire alongside its frontier, the river Danube. Tacitus, in "The Annals" (page 17) says,

232

"The Eighth and Fifteenth Legions were actually ready to fight each other, the one demanding the execution of a man named Sirpicus, and the men of the Fifteenth sheltering him; but the soldiers of the Ninth Legion intervened with appeals, and threats when they were ignored."

In AD20 the Legion was temporarily moved to North Africa to quell the uprising led by Tacfarinas, a Numidian who had deserted from the army. Eventually he was defeated. Tacitus (pages 148 to 149) says,

"That year [AD24] finally released the Roman people from the long drawn out war against the Numidian Tacfarinas ... the emperor had ordered that the Ninth Legion be brought home, as if there were no longer enemies in Africa."

So the Legion ended back on the Danube despite continuing unrest in Africa, remaining there until Aulus Plautius put together his invasion force in AD43.

I then followed in the footsteps of the Ninth Legion. They arrived in Richborough and advanced to Colchester in AD43. Prior to the Boudiccan revolt of AD60/61 when the Legion was almost wiped out, it had set up its base in Lincoln. It was eventually made back up to strength and by AD71 had reached York. After the quelling of the Brigantes the Legion went through a sustained period of stability. Peter Salway in "The Oxford Illustrated History of Roman Britain" (page 108) says,

"Early in the second century the long series of changes in the location of legions in Britain was over. Henceforth, for a century or more, there were three permanent fortresses at Chester, Caerleon and York, occupied at this time by the Twentieth, II Augusta and the Ninth respectively."

As to the Legion's disappearance from history, we have got fiction writer Rosemary Sutcliffe to thank (or blame) for the ongoing myth that the Ninth Legion was obliterated during a campaign in northern Britain. Whilst her book, "The Eagle of the Ninth" (published in 1954), is a splendid adventure yarn aimed at children, there is no truth in the story of the Legion's demise. The film, "The Eagle" (2011), is based on Sutcliffe's book. Sadly, in that rather dreary film we see Celtic chariots incorrectly pictured with scythes on their wheels.

We have fairly conclusive evidence that the Legion was still in York as late as AD108. Part of a tablet found there in the mid-19th century says,

> "The Emperor Caesar Nerva Trajan Augustus, son of the deified Nerva, Conqueror of Germany, Conqueror of Dacia, pontifex maximus, in his twelfth year of tribunician power, six times acclaimed emperor, five times consul, father of his country, built this gate by the agency of the Ninth Legion Hispana."

This tablet commemorated the building of a gateway into the city. A roof tile found in Nijmegen in 1959 is thought to point to the Ninth Legion being based at the military camp there in the second century. However, the evidence is not conclusive and the actual age of the tile is uncertain.

We are then left with conjecture. The Ninth Legion may have been withdrawn from Britain prior to the commencement of the building of Hadrian's Wall (started in AD122). However, as so many soldiers would have been involved in the wall building programme, the Legion could have returned temporarily. Salway says (page 127),

> "There is even a possibility that the Ninth returned for a while, temporarily restoring the legionary garrison to four during the period when there was great pressure on military resources from the building programme on the Wall."

As to the Legion's eventual fate, Salway adds (page 127),

> "It has been conjectured that it [the Ninth Legion] was eventually lost in the east, long after its final withdrawal from Britain."

By the mid second century however, we do know that there is strong evidence for the non-existence of the Legion. In around AD165 the Emperor, Marcus Aurelius, commissioned some columns which detailed every legion and its location in the Empire. There is no mention of the Ninth Legion on any of the columns. Annihilation in a conflict in the east of the Roman Empire? Broken up and the soldiers transferred to other legions to make up the numbers? We do not know for certain. Sheppard Frere sums it up succinctly in "Britannia, a History of Roman Britain" (page 124),

> "Further evidence is needed before more can be said"

So I will say no more.

14 YORK (EBURACUM)

Over the centuries York has been the centre of a number of tribes, races and jurisdictions. In simple terms, the Celts were conquered by the Romans who then left, their place being taken by the Anglo Saxon invaders from mainland Europe, who in turn were then replaced by the Vikings from northern Europe. The Vikings were eventually forced out by the Anglo Saxons. Then it was the turn of the Normans.

As mentioned in the previous chapter, the Ninth Legion built the fortress at York in around AD71. Prior to that it was not only the Boudiccan revolt that had slowed the progress of the Romans, and reduced the military capacity of the Legion, but events back home had taken centre stage. As Patricia Southern in "Roman Britain, A New History 55BC-AD450" (page 119) says,

> *"In AD69, when British civic and commercial life may have been reviving, the Roman world lurched into a home-made crisis, and everything was put on hold."*

This crisis became known as the year of the four emperors. Emperor Nero was hated by all classes of society and yet there was no unifying cause to oust him. In AD68 he committed suicide and the Spanish troops appointed their governor, Galba, as emperor. On his arrival in Rome Galba received the support of the Praetorian Guard and was formally proclaimed as emperor (number 1). Early in AD69 the Pretorian Guard changed allegiance, killed Galba, and put Otho in his place (number 2). A few days before this, troops in Germany announced that their choice for emperor was Vitellius (number 3). Otho's army was defeated at the battle of Bedriacum after which he committed suicide.

Here is where the British connection comes in; the three legions in Britain favoured Vitellius and 8,000 troops were withdrawn from the island to support his cause. Cartimandua, the pro-Roman client queen of the Brigantes, had previously divorced her husband Venutius. Seeing that the Romans were looking towards Rome, Venutius felt the time was right to fight against his former wife. The Romans did not have sufficient troops to support Cartimandua so were left with no alternative but to leave Venutius, an anti-Roman, as the new leader of the Brigantes.

Now we come to emperor number 4, and one of the great Roman emperors. Titus Flavius Vespasianus (Vespasian) had been one of the generals in Aulus Plautius' invading army of Britain in AD43. Sometime after having lead a successful conquest of part of the west of the island he was recalled to Rome. It is believed that he then fell foul of Nero. Patricia Southern suggests (page 121),

> *"Vespasianus had been appointed governor of Judaea, in the latter half of AD66, to quell the revolt that had broken out there. It was said that Vespasian had committed the unforgivable error of dozing off, probably bored out of his mind, while Nero was reciting poems on his literary tour of Greece."*

On hearing that Galba had been killed, Vespasian was declared emperor by the legions in Egypt and Judaea. Troops loyal to Vespasian defeated those of Vitellius at the battle of Cremona. Thus began the Flavian dynasty from AD 69 to 96, with Vespasian (69 to 79), and his two sons, Titus (79 to 81) and Domitian (81 to 96). It is during this time that the Romanisation of Britain gathered pace. Most of the rest of the island was conquered and towns and countryside flourished. Interestingly, most of the remains of the grand Roman buildings that have been unearthed in Britain date from the Flavian period.

Once the role of Emperor was sorted out, the continuation of the conquest of Britain could be considered. North of the Humber were two tribes; the Brigantes in what became Lancashire, Cumbria and west Yorkshire, and the Parisi tribe in east Yorkshire. The fort at Malton was set up to keep an eye on the latter tribe, which saw the benefits of maintaining friendly relations with their conquerors. For many years the client queen of the Brigantes, Cartimandua, had ensured that there was a peaceful ally on the northwest border of the Empire. Unfortunately, the defeat of Cartimandua by her ex-husband signalled a rise in opposition from the Brigantes. Cerialis, who had been the legate of the Ninth Legion when it was defeated by the Iceni, became governor of Britannia in AD71. Patricia Southern says (page 125),

> *"The situation that Cerialis inherited was somewhat threatening, since the Brigantes were no longer ruled by the pro-Roman Queen Cartimandua. Her husband Venutius had been left in charge and there was probably no shortage of anti-Roman warriors who would rally around Venutius if he decided to go to war."*

There were a number of small turf and timber forts that flanked the edges of the Brigantes' territory. However, Cerialis was no longer content with policing, especially as the Brigantes seemed to be spoiling for a fight. As Southern says (page 125),

> *"With Cerialis' arrival, Roman policy changed from one of containment to active invasion."*

Thus, in the year he became governor, the Ninth Legion was sent to York and the Roman fortress was founded. From here, the conquest of northern Britain would take place, eventually reaching as far as the Moray Firth in northern Scotland. But that is, as they say, another story. Suffice to say, York became one of the major military and then civilian towns of Roman Britain.

The fortress was built in the triangular area that had the river Ouse on the left and the river Foss on the right. This easily defended position had access to the North Sea via the Ouse. The colonia was established on the other side of the rivers, to the south. It eventually became the capital of Britannia Inferior, the northern province; two having been created in the early 3rd century. All of the public buildings, shops and houses associated with coloniae would have been built in York. It is even believed that a temple was erected at which the imperial cult was observed.

With the arrival of the Romans, trade soon flourished, and not just by the locals. In York there is evidence of merchants from the continent being drawn to the colonia. A tradesman, M. Verecundius Diogenes from Bourges in France, set up his business in York. Another Frenchman, L. Viducius Placidus from Rouen, had a shrine erected in the town.

In the early second century, the Ninth Legion was replaced by the Sixth Legion, the latter using York as its base until the Romans departed from Britain in AD410. We do not know why the Legion was replaced and even more mysterious is the fact that after AD117 no further reference to it has been uncovered. I have already delved into possible reasons for its disappearance from history in the previous chapter and can fairly confidently say that abduction by aliens was not the cause.

Something that happened in York that did not in any other Roman town in Britannia is that two emperors died there. Septimus Severus was emperor from AD193 to 211. During his reign he was responsible for expanding the Empire to its greatest limits. The final part of his activity was in Britannia. He strengthened Hadrian's Wall and even reoccupied the Antonine Wall; the latter (between modern day Glasgow and Edinburgh) had been built by AD154, but only eight years later was abandoned when the Romans fell back to the line of Hadrian's Wall. Severus' final expansion in Britannia was curtailed when he died at York in AD211. Shortly afterwards the army in Caledonia (Scotland) withdrew for the final time to Hadrian's Wall.

Almost 100 years later, the emperor Constantius led a successful war against the Picts to the north of the Antonine Wall in AD305. He died suddenly the following year in York. On his death his son Constantine was declared Emperor. He is the first emperor who converted to Christianity in AD312, although this did not become the state religion until AD391.

***

As mentioned at the start of the chapter, alongside the Roman link with York one should also consider other historical associations with the city; Anglo Saxons, Vikings, Normans, the Wars of the Roses and the English Civil War. It was 400 years after the Romans left York that the Vikings arrived. During the intervening period the Anglo Saxons steadily built up a presence in the area. These people would have originally been mercenaries linked to the Roman army but then their number was supplemented by migration from Europe. The darkly lit history of the period is illuminated by two major works of literature. The first, "The Ecclesiastical History of the English People", was completed around AD731 by Bede. When considering its credibility one should remember that it is a mixture of facts and legends and written a long time after the events that are described. Bede was a devout Christian and as such the religious importance of the events is key in his writings. The second oft quoted text is the "Anglo-Saxon Chronicle", a late ninth century work written during the reign of Alfred the Great. Whilst there is little reference to York in the early years after the Romans (called the sub Roman period), we do know that in the seventh century the first minster was built to baptise Edwin of Deira, king of Northumbria. This was built of wood and no evidence of its presence survives, but it is believed to have been built where the current minster stands. York became renowned throughout Europe as a centre of the faith, second only in importance to Canterbury. The first Archbishop of York, Egbert, oversaw the building of a superb cathedral when the previous one burnt down in 741. Because the Anglo Saxons built mainly in wood, little if any of their structures can be seen in modern day York.

The Anglo Saxon prosperity that York enjoyed eventually became threatened and then replaced by the invasion of the Vikings. These sea-borne Scandinavians may have started out as mere pirates, invading and plundering the rich towns and fertile countryside of eastern and northern Britain. However, after about 100 years of these seemingly uncoordinated raids, in the 9th century the Vikings became not only conquerors but explorers and settlers. These were not primitive warriors but farmers and fishermen with skills and their own religious beliefs. They sought new lands to enrich their lives. The Viking army attacked York in November 866, wintered on the Tyne, and then retook the city in March 867. The "Anglo Saxon Chronicle" wrote that there was "an excessive slaughter of the Northumbrians", including the killing of local kings, Aelle and Osbert. Two years later the Danelaw was formed. King Alfred of Wessex (he who has gone down in history as a great monarch but poor chef, having allegedly burnt some cakes) agreed a truce with the Vikings whereby England was divided into the Anglo Saxon south and the Viking north. Their capital city was set up in York, named Jorvik by the invaders. The town became an important river port with trade links to mainland Europe.

I love Viking names. The person who led their original attack on York in 866 was Ivar the Boneless. When they were eventually expelled in 954 their leader was Eric Bloodaxe. (On a lighter note, don't forget Oliver Postgate's Nordic saga of Noggin the Nog and Nogbad the Bad.) In the intervening period, Jorvik became home to great craftsmen, traders, artists and ship builders. Like the Anglo Saxons, the Vikings built their shops and houses out of wood. Unlike the Anglo Saxons, archaeologists have found much evidence of the Viking presence; jewellery, wood carvings, textiles. Many were Christians too and they built churches, including St Olave's on Marygate and St Mary on Bishopshill. The term gate is a reference to the Viking word for street. This can be confusing when we think of the term gate to mean an entrance.

Eventually the Anglo Saxons became strong enough to force out the Vikings from the Danelaw and so the stage was set for the next invaders, the Normans. In the previous chapter I mentioned in some detail the battle of Stamford Bridge in September 1066, where Saxon King Harold defeated an attempted invasion by the Norseman Harold Hardrada. This was the precursor to the battle of Hastings in October of the same year which saw the introduction of the Normans to Britain.

In 1068 William, now king of England and not just conqueror, marched on York. It was seen as a potential centre of discontent and rebellion. As a mark of his authority William ordered the construction of two castles in the York area; London being the only other town to have two Norman castles. These castles, at Clifford's Tower and Baille Hill, were designed to control entry to the city via the river Ouse. In 1069 a local uprising was put down with extreme viciousness. However, a similar fate was meted out to the Normans later in the year when King Swein the Dane arrived with a large fleet of ships and, allied with the local Anglo Saxons, burned the castles and Minster to the ground and massacred the Normans. On hearing of this, William paid off the Danes who left the town to allow William to take his revenge, with many thousands dying from violence and famine. The castles and the Minster were rebuilt. Over the next few years many churches and an Abbey, St Mary's, were constructed. Despite his violent tendency, William was a deeply religious man.

My apologies for this paragraph, lots of kings, many confusingly named Edward, and numerous dates to trudge through. For the next 400 years York prospered, benefitting from a long period of relative peace. In 1212 King John granted the city a charter whereby the locals became responsible for raising taxes. For a brief period of time Edward I moved the centre of the national government to York (1298-1304) and based his army there during his war on the Scots. Both he and his son, Edward II failed to quell the Scots. Following the English army's defeat at Bannockburn in 1314, there was concern that the Scots would attack York. These fears of attack were only relieved in 1323 when Edward II concluded a truce with Robert the Bruce at Bishopthorpe in York. Edward's son, Edward III, continued the royal links with York. He was married at the Minster in 1328 and moved the centre of government to York. Between 1298 and 1335 parliament met 15 times in the city. Richard II, the last Plantagenet king of England, succeeded Edward III as king and created the title Duke of York for his uncle. In 1399 Henry of Lancaster usurped the throne from Richard, becoming Henry IV, and so set the scene for the Wars of the Roses (York white, Lancaster red).

Both the houses of York and Lancaster could trace their rights to kingship back to a common ancestor, Edward III. Then again most people could probably trace their ancestry back to him as he had 14 children. For thirty years (1455-1485) the Wars of the Roses saw the throne of England seesaw between both royal houses.

It was only when the Yorkist Richard III was defeated by the Lancastrian Henry Tudor (becoming Henry VII, the father of Henry VIII) that the war ended. Richard had visited York on a number of occasions, including being crowned Prince of Wales there. There are museums dedicated to both Richard III and Henry VII in York. Rather oddly, they are not called museums but "Richard III Experience" and "Henry VII Experience". Is this an attempt to try to make history trendy?

The Wars of the Roses pre-empted the English Civil War in that the conflict lasted many years and bloody battles were fought at different locations, including St Albans, Barnet, Towton, Ferrybridge and finally at Bosworth in Leicestershire. The big difference between these two civil wars is that the first was a dynastic conflict to determine who would rule the nation whereas the second was a struggle to determine how the nation would be ruled.

Henry VII's son, Henry VIII (he of the six wives) also has a link with York via the Pilgrimage of Grace, the only rebellion against the monarch during his reign. As part of the dissolution of the monasteries, Roman Catholic monasteries, priories and convents were systematically disbanded and looted. The reason given for this was the alleged corruption of these institutions. The treasures, money and land confiscated became useful in swelling the coffers of Henry's treasury, especially to fund a potential war with France. The dissolution also reinforced Henry's break from Rome following his divorce from his first wife, Catherine of Aragon. Northern Catholics, angered by the treatment of members of their religion and other economic issues, rebelled in 1536, their leader being a lawyer, Robert Aske. A band of 9,000 peaceful rebels occupied York in a symbolic rather than aggressive gesture. At no point were any battles or fights recorded. Near Doncaster, Henry's representative the duke of Norfolk negotiated with Aske. By this time 40,000 people had joined this popular uprising. On being given assurances that their grievances would be looked into, Aske disbanded his followers. In February 1537, a further rebellion took place in modern day Cumbria. Aske was not a member of this. Henry decided that negotiation was no longer a possibility so had the leaders arrested and executed (including Aske). At York castle Aske was hanged, drawn and quartered following a trial. The uprising petered out.

During the civil war (1642 to 1651) between the royalist supporters of Charles I and the Parliamentarians, York again became a focal point. Escaping the London mob in 1642, Charles I moved his family and court to the city. For six months York became the capital of the kingdom. Charles left York in August to raise his standard in Nottingham, thus signifying the start of the civil war. Prior to that the city walls were repaired in anticipation of an impending conflict. The city avoided any major involvement in the war until the Parliamentarians' victory at nearby Selby in April 1644. Under constant bombardment the defenders were forced to retreat inside the city walls. It was not until one of the pivotal battles of the civil war at nearby Marston Moor where the Parliamentarians secured a decisive victory (July 1644) that the people of York realised that further defence of the city was useless. A few days after the battle, articles of surrender were agreed. An important proclamation was made which has benefited the city to this day. The parliamentarian leader, Sir Thomas Fairfax, said that there would be no ransacking or destruction of the city's churches. Even the Minster's stained glass was to remain untouched.

With this, York's long history as a fortress and military headquarters drew to a close. The Romans had set up a base here in AD71 and the Royalists relinquished theirs in 1644. The city could now focus on its role as a centre of local government and trade and become one of the country's leading tourist attractions.

***

And it was my turn to be a tourist and visit many of the attractions. As with my trip around Lincoln, I was expecting great things of York; one of the major Roman towns and, in later years, a huge Viking settlement, Norman city and centre of one of the royal houses in the Wars of the Roses. One thing different to Lincoln is the importance of the Roman road. Ermine Street runs from south to north in a straight line through Lincoln. Most of the sites I had visited there had been either on the line of Ermine Street or ever so slightly to the left (castle) or right (cathedral). The ridge was the dominant geographical feature, with the river Witham playing a subsidiary role. In York it was the rivers Ouse and Foss that were at the heart of the city. I had been able to "do" Lincoln in one day but needed to allow myself two to get round most of the sites of York.

Unlike Lincoln, with the best examples of sewers in the province, the Romans seem to have been less efficient when it came to York. Commenting on the sewage system, Lindsay Allason-Jones in "Women in Roman Britain" (page 77) says that,

> *"However, the rough sides of the main drains at York would have been difficult to flush clean and in the summer the amount of water available may well have been inadequate."*

Thankfully, the drains in modern York did seem to be coping and I could not detect any organic aromas. In preparation for my walk I had read Charlotte Higgins book "Under Another Sky, Journeys in Roman Britain". In this excellent volume she describes the Roman involvement in places she visited. Chapter 9 (pages 161 to 178) gives a detailed history of York.

My plan was to walk from my hotel to the city wall and on day one walk westwards around the wall and on day two eastwards. I set off from my hotel and arrived at Micklegate Bar (see below), one of the entrances to the walled city which also housed the Henry VII Experience. Here, I noted that the city drains were a topic of conversation. A plaque said,

"During the reign of Henry VII, the paved streets of York had open gutters running through them and the city was notoriously dirty and smelly."

Phew. So, not much change to Roman times. According to the York civic record of 1501 (their spelling, not mine),

"there shal be a dung cart in every ward to take refuse out of the city where it should be layd so that husbands of the countrie may come there to have it away."

Obviously, "having it away" meant something slightly different to what it means today, unless the Tudor gentlemen were somewhat kinky.

I walked along the wall, crossed the river Ouse and arrived at the Museum Gardens. Here I saw a structure that I could immediately tell was of Roman origin (layers of red bricks). This is the remains of the west corner of the Roman fort.

In the gardens of the museum were the ruins of St Mary's Abbey. Once the richest abbey in the north of England, St Mary's fell foul to the dissolution of the monasteries in 1539. Another attractive building in the museum grounds was a 14th house, the Hospitium, which is now hired out for weddings. It used to be the place where lower ranking visitors to the abbey were put up for the night.

Inside, the museum was a veritable treasure trove of Roman relics and other more modern artefacts, all painstakingly laid out and identified. One tombstone was particularly moving. A script by the side said,

> "This tombstone tells the story of a real human tragedy. Caeresius Augustinus, an ex-soldier, suffered the loss of two infant children and his wife, Flavia Augustina. Here they are shown much older, perhaps demonstrating their father's aspirations for how they might grow up."

There was a large mosaic floor with a sign that said you had to take your shoes off if you wanted to walk on it. I could not remember if I had holes in my socks so just looked at the mosaic rather than walk on it.

The museum and its grounds are a wonderful space. Many families were taking advantage of the lovely early spring weather and were wandering around the gardens and abbey ruins. It then occurred to me that, even for those who cannot afford the entry prices of the many places to visit in York, there are enough sights to view and walk through, including the wall, where no entry fee is required.

And then I arrived at the Minster. The first thing I needed to clarify was why is it called York Minster and not York Cathedral? Apparently, a minster is not necessarily the same as a cathedral. A minster is a church that was established in Anglo-Saxon times as a missionary teaching church or a church attached to a monastery. If the minster then houses the place where a bishop is based it is called a cathedral (cathedra being the name for the bishop's throne). So, a minster may not be a cathedral and a cathedral may not be a minster. In York's case it is both a minster and cathedral. My head is starting to hurt now so I am going to make a coffee.

As in the case of Lincoln cathedral, York is huge and was difficult to photograph to get an appreciation of its true scale. Even taken from the city wall it was hard to appreciate its size. For all the medieval grandeur I found the most moving image inside to be a large modern mock-up of the crucifixion and resurrection of Christ; the essence of Christianity.

On leaving the Minster/Cathedral I stumbled upon two Roman artefacts; a statue of Constantine, the first Roman emperor to be converted to Christianity, and an oddly placed column (see both below). I say oddly placed because it just appeared to be stuck in the street, not supporting a building. My research suggests that it originated in the north-east colonnade of the Roman headquarters. Originally built by the Ninth Legion in AD100 it was rediscovered by archaeologists beneath York minster, rebuilt and placed in its current location in 1971.

My last visit of day one was to the Treasurer's House close to the Minster. This used to be the place where the treasurer for York Minster resided. It is now a National Trust property, having been bequeathed to them by Frank Green in 1930.

Green was a wealthy industrialist. Having walked through the house and read various documents there I also think he could have had a screw loose (more of that in a minute). During restoration work carried out by Green, four Roman column bases were uncovered. The house was built on top of the site of one of the Roman roads leading out of the city. A party guest of Green saw some Roman soldiers in the cellar. One could blame the party spirit for that but not for the next sighting of this ghostly apparition. In 1953 during restoration work being done by the National Trust, an apprentice plumber saw Roman soldiers in the cellar and described what they were wearing. As this didn't fit in with the standard uniform known at the time his claim was dismissed. Years later, evidence was unearthed that suggests that the type of uniform he described was actually worn by Roman soldiers in Britain. Cellar tours are available on request. I was too busy to go down into the cellar, ahem.

Anyway, back to Green and his loose screw, or should I say loose stud? When he bequeathed the property and contents to the National Trust he said that no furniture should be moved out of place. He had small studs (some of which you can still see) nailed into the floorboards to mark the position of the furniture. He threatened to haunt the house were any items to be moved. Despite being a generous man he was ill-tempered with staff and colleagues. It is said that on one occasion he saw a fly in the kitchen and so ordered all food in the house to be destroyed. Not surprisingly he remained a bachelor all his life. I went back to my hotel and happily rearranged some of the furniture in my room just because I could.

It had rained during the night but yet again I was blessed with good weather for the next day's ramble. I aimed for the Micklegate Bar but this time having reached it I went east along the wall. The original Roman wall (of which I had seen part of in the museum grounds the previous day) would have been totally inside the area north of the rivers Ouse and Foss. The later wall, of which much remains to this day, extends south of the river Ouse as well as north. There are more miles of walkable wall in York than any other place in England and I walked most of them. I noticed the same camaraderie on the wall that I come across when walking the fells. People who pass each other say hello. If I had passed the same people on the streets of York there would have been no cheery salutation.

The wall has four main gatehouses, known as bars (Bootham, Monk, Walmgate and Micklegate). As well as defensive places, these gates would have been used to extract tolls from people seeking entry to the city. Fishergate bar and Victoria bar are two minor gates in the wall.

The wall stops abruptly when it reaches the river Ouse. The river is navigable throughout its whole length (52 miles) Add on the part called the river Ure and it is 129 miles and the sixth longest in the United Kingdom. Its link to the Humber and North Sea is what helped York to become the major city it did. Today York is home to riverboat cruisers and a rowing club.

I made my way around the east and north of the city, using both the wall and streets, until I reached Monk Bar. This is home to the Richard III Experience and I experienced it. If you remember, he was the Yorkist king who was defeated as the battle of Bosworth by Henry Tudor, thus ending the Wars of the Roses. It was here that I learnt about the battle of Towton, not only the bloodiest battle of the war but also the one with the greatest loss of British life in one day in a conflict. In October 1066, the battle of Hastings saw around 10,000 deaths, a mixture of English and Normans. On the first day of the Somme in July 2016, 19,000 British and Empire soldiers died. At Towton, in March 1461, it is believed that 28,000 Englishmen died, mainly Lancastrians. Most of these were killed during the rout of the Lancastrians as each side had decided that no quarter would be given. The battle was fought during a snowstorm with the blizzard driving the snow and arrows into the Lancastrians faces.

Cautious note: A greater loss of British dead in one day is mentioned by Tacitus. In chapter 12, when discussing the Boudiccan revolt, he is recorded as saying that her army was finally defeated with a loss of 80,000 Britons. This is probably an exaggerated figure to make the Roman victory appear even more impressive than it actually was.

With that sobering thought I made my way to Barley Hall. This place is one of York's great restoration successes. As late as the 1980's it was hidden under a derelict office block. With time and attention to detail the York Archaeological Trust has painstakingly researched into the old building and rebuilt it, using original parts of the structure wherever possible. Well done them.

It was getting close to lunchtime so I needed to make my way to York's Chocolate Story. This tour celebrates York's historical links to chocolate and sweets. Using much hands on experience (well, eating lots of samples actually) I learnt about the Terrys, Rowntrees and Cravens. I even made and ate my own lollipop. It was great fun, with much of the enjoyment coming from the enthusiastic and knowledgeable tour guide (and the chocolate).

Just around the corner from the tour I stumbled across the Shambles. This is a quaint narrow street full of old world charm. The name Shambles has nothing to do with the place looking a mess. Previously known as the Great Flesh Shambles (Anglo Saxon for shelves) the street housed many butchers with their shelves of meat. I walked down the street peering into the shops then walked back up again and bought two pork and black pudding pies for my tea (and very tasty they were too).

I suppose anyone going to York these days has to pay a visit to the Jorvik centre. This place celebrates York's Viking past. You sit in a little car which transports you from one Viking scene to another whilst a commentary gives you plenty of detail. The dummies are very life like. After the ride there is a mini museum to wander around. I particularly liked the video that demonstrated musical instruments the Vikings would have used. About ten years ago I went there with my daughter. Having visited it again I sent her a text saying that it had not changed one bit. She replied by suggesting that the Vikings hadn't done much in the last ten years to warrant the exhibition needing an update. She has a point.

There were two more places I wanted to see before I made my way back to the hotel. Firstly, I went to the Castle Museum, or to be precise, the place where one of the castles used to be. The museum is housed in the old female prison. Inside I found an eclectic mix of memorabilia from the 19th and 20th centuries. The star of the show was definitely the full scale mock-up of a Victorian street. It was great fun wandering in and out of the shops.

My final stop was the Clifford's Tower which contained an English Heritage mock-up of what the castle and grounds would have looked like.

The first castle was built here in 1068 by William the Conqueror to a standard motte and bailey design; the motte being Clifford's Tower and the bailey the flat area to the right of the motte. The moat around the motte was formed by diverting part of the river Foss. As befits such a prominent landmark in York, the Tower had a varied and often gruesome history. The Danes (remember Swein the Dane?) destroyed much of the building. On their departure it was rebuilt.

In March 1190 an infamous event took place. Following the coronation of Richard I, it was falsely rumoured that he had ordered the massacre of Jews. This was the time of the Crusades around Jerusalem and not only were Muslims seen as the enemy but also the Jews. 150 Jews were given protective custody in Clifford's Tower. Probably due to confusion it was decided to force them out of the Tower. Anticipating that they would be murdered on their removal, the Jews set fire to the roof and attempted suicide. Those that survived were taken from the Tower and murdered. Jewish life eventually revived in York but 100 years later, in 1290, Edward I expelled all Jews from England.

A sturdy stone castle eventually replaced the old one but even that slowly decayed and became a ruin as the site was not used as a royal residence. It is not certain where the name Clifford comes from. Two contenders stand out as possibilities. The Clifford family (constables of the area) may have seen it as their property. Or it may get its name from Roger de Clifford who was hanged there in 1322. During the civil war the Tower was firstly occupied by Royalists and then by Parliamentarians. Its final ignominy came in 1684 when, during a ceremony to celebrate St George's day, the roof ignited during the firing of cannon and was never repaired. The Tower then was looked on as a folly by the townsfolk. The rest of the castle area (the bailey) was developed as a prison. Eventually this was dismantled and the modern buildings erected.

I appreciate that I did not visit all of York's historic sites and tourist attractions. If I were to have another day in the city I would seek out the National Railway Museum, York Art Gallery, the York Dungeon, Fairfax House and the Merchant Adventurers Hall. As it is, I had found York to have been one of the most interesting cities that I have ever visited, both at home and abroad. At the end of two very tiring but enjoyable and educational days wandering around historic York, I made my way to the train station for my trip home.

My modern Roman road trip had literally come to the end of the road, that road being Ermine Street. The first place that I had visited on my walk was an English Heritage site, Richborough fort in Kent; so was the last one, Clifford's Tower in Yorkshire. And I like that bookending of my Roman road trip very much.

15 WHERE TO END?

So, that makes the journey from Richborough to York, including the detour to Colchester, a total of 305 miles. To get back home from York, for the same price rail ticket I could go one of two routes; York via Manchester to Penrith, or York via Leeds via Lancaster to Penrith (both routes about 170 miles). I did the first option. Getting from Penrith to Sandwich right at the start of my Roman road trip had been around 370 miles.

During my extended walk I had visited 7 of the 24 main Roman towns in Britain (in itinerary order; Canterbury, London, Colchester, Water Newton, Lincoln, Brough-on-Humber, York). As to Roman roads, I had followed a minor one from Richborough to Canterbury (Margary 10), the southern part of Watling Street (Margary 1) from Canterbury to London, another major road from London to Colchester (Margary 3), and all of Ermine Street (Margary 2). I hadn't touched the third major Roman road, Fosse Way, other than give it a brief hello in Lincoln. And the librarian in Penrith will be disappointed to know that I only mentioned Hadrian's Wall a handful of times.

To be honest, I had only scratched the surface of the Roman road network in Britain, a network that was primarily built over virgin terrain. As Philip Wilkinson says in "What the Romans Did for Us" (page 42),

> *"It has been estimated that the Romans built well over 10,000 miles of roads while they occupied Britain. Some of these were based on the earlier prehistoric tracks, such as the ridgeways that ran along the crests of hills, and other routes connecting hill forts. But more often, especially when it came*

to the great long-distance routes, the Romans were covering
new ground, surveying and building from scratch."

The roads were built to aid conquest and then consolidation and communication. The invaders knew the importance of these vital arteries along which troops, trade and taxes flowed. Margary (page 496) says,

"Military requirements undoubtedly influenced the layout of
most of the main routes, but many of the branch roads would
have been added later to meet commercial and local
requirements as the province became peacefully settled and
the market towns and farming and mining areas were
established."

Viewed alongside the great high profile engineering projects whose ruins are in evidence today (temples, aqueducts, amphitheatres and other popular tourist attractions) throughout the old Roman Empire, the humble Roman road never gets a first, let alone second glance. And yet the legacy of these once great highways is as clear today as any of the must see relics of past glory. As Wilkinson says (page 41),

"The work of the Roman civil engineers had a lasting impact;
the imprint of their roads is still obvious all over the British
landscape, in the form of the modern roads that follow the
tracks of Roman ones."

I witnessed that in Kent (A2), Essex (A12), North of London (A10), through Cambridgeshire (A1 and A1M) and Lincolnshire (A15). At times I had been creative with my journey planning so as to avoid becoming road kill on one of the major trunk routes. And as to that fiendish B2000 near Cooling in Kent, I still get nightmares. Of the major Roman roads that I did not encounter, the mighty A5 follows the line of Watling Street north of London and Fosse Way is the blue print for major roads between Exeter and Lincoln. Then there are the countless old Roman roads that have been built over that link modern towns and villages.

The Romans built a systematic network of routes that helped to unify the country during their occupation, and with some of them ending up at coastal forts and towns, linked Britain to its continental neighbours in a more efficient manner than had previously been the case. Eventually, these roads helped to forge an identity that the Celtic tribes and their informal paths and communities were not able to do. Once the Romans left these shores their criss-cross communication network ensured that those that followed in their footsteps would have a template already made to smooth the path to becoming a nation. And this, rather than the ruined forts, towns and villas, is their true legacy to Britain.

That the definite routes of many old Roman roads have been lost to us should come as no surprise. Due to changing demands some early roads would have outlived their usefulness, even during the occupation. It is not testimony of bad engineering that is to blame for their loss but the power of plant colonisation. How often have you walked down a minor, metalled country lane and seen the road clearly delineated by the tracks of the tyres and yet in the middle of the road, and at the edges, vegetation has taken hold? Were vehicles to stop using the road altogether it would not be long before it would be overgrown and then the effects of biological weathering would disintegrate the tarmac.

Throughout my journey I had used Margary's "Roman Roads in Britain" as my key reference with regards to the Roman road network. I would literally have been lost without it. At this point, for the sake of completion, I should mention two other reference works on the routes of Roman roads. These other two are classical sources and have far less detail than Margary goes into and, as far as my requirements were concerned, of little but historical value. Of the first Margary says (page 27),

> "By far the most valuable source is the Itinerary of Antoninus; this is generally considered to date from the end of the second or the beginning of the third century, and is really a route-book giving lists of places and the distance between them in miles."

In M.C. Bishop's "The Secret History of the Roman Roads of Britain" (page 48), a map of the Antonine Itinerary in England and Wales is reprinted. This section is called the Iter Britanniarum and covers 15 routes. If I were to walk the Roman roads of the continent then I would probably start out with the Antonine Itinerary. This document lists the towns, villages and mail stations throughout the Roman Empire. There is some debate as to the naming of it; it may or may not be named after Antoninus, he who had the Antonine Wall built across the central belt in Scotland.

Margary also refers to the second source (page 27),

> "A rather similar record [to the Antonine Itinerary], but in the form of a diagrammatic sketch-map, is provided by the Tabula Peutingeriana, the original of which is believed to date from the third century. On the thirteenth century copy, which is all that has survived, the Roman Empire is depicted upon a number of parchment sheets fastened together as a long roll; unfortunately most of Britain came upon the outermost sheet, which is lost."

The thirteenth century copy is in the Austrian National Library in Vienna. In honour of its antiquity and value, it was placed on UNESCO's "Memory of the World Register" in 2007. This is part of an international programme to safeguard items that according to UNESCO, "transcend the boundaries of time and culture". In this version of the Tabula Peutingeriana, a sketchy and inaccurate outline of some roads in the Southeast and East Anglia survives.

The weather had been extremely kind to me considering that I made my trip during October to November and March to April. I could only remember three days of serious downpours; in Kent (Rainham) and Cambridgeshire (Papworth Everard and Huntingdon). Apart from that the late autumnal and early spring weather had been blessed with a fair degree of sunshine. And, other than the weather, what was the one abiding memory of my road trip through rural, and occasionally urban, England? It has to be the number of places of worship dedicated to Christianity. I had visited major cathedrals (Canterbury, St Paul's in London, Chelmsford, Lincoln and York) and wondered at their majesty and glorification of the Christian God. Then in every village I passed through I saw churches, some now defunct but most still places of worship. Whether you are a believer or not I would recommend calling in to some of these places. One cannot help but get a sense of tranquillity in them.

And the most thought provoking place I have been to? This is an easy one to answer. When I started in Sandwich and first arrived at Richborough I thought that this would be the most amazing place that I would see; it was an extremely evocative place, especially in the early morning light of an October morning. It is a rarely visited spot that was key to the Romans' four centuries of rule of Britannia; the Romans who, with their legacy of a road network, helped to define the future of this Island even long after they left these shores. Then again, at the end of my trip, York was probably the most historic place I have ever been to (in this country or abroad) and was involved in each epoch in terms of the evolution of this Island's identity. The city seems to have been involved in all the major conflicts and developments that shaped the Englishness that is part of my life.

But neither Richborough nor York is the most thought provoking place. That honour has to go to St Martin's, the small non-descript church on the outskirts of Canterbury, that just happens to have been the first Christian church founded on this Island and the oldest parish church still in use. If you look closely you can still see the small red bricks that would have been made by the Romans and used in their original town of Durovernum Cantiacorum and then used as spoila when incorporated into the structure of the church.

It is not the bricks that give one pause for thought, nor that the church is part of the Canterbury World Heritage Site (along with its more illustrious neighbours, St Augustine's Priory and

Canterbury Cathedral). It is what the tiny parish church represents in terms of the nation's identity. Once the Roman Emperor Constantine converted to Christianity, this religion was slowly taken on board by succeeding generations of Romans, Anglo Saxons, Vikings, Normans and later royal households. Throughout that time it drove the actions of both nobles and simple country folk alike. St Martin's was there at the beginning of the transition from a pagan nation to a belief in a Christian God. This belief and the Roman road network helped to shape the land and people that evolved from Celtic Britannia into modern Great Britain.

I was brought up a Roman Catholic and still believe that Jesus Christ is a pretty good role model for how to behave even though a belief in a God and eternal salvation gets harder over time.

***

So, where to end? Whilst on my travels I have talked about the Romans in Britain during the conquest. Also, I have picked out elements of English history, both major and minor and also downright loopy, that related to places I passed through. Occasionally, I have included some personal reminiscences that places stirred in me. I currently live in Cumbria and previously have spent a number of years working there and in Scotland; times full of happy memories. I have had some wonderful holidays beyond Hadrian's Wall and even went to the Highlands on my honeymoon. Each year, around Easter, I spend an idyllic week in a cottage in the Borders in a tiny village called Ashkirk with my sister Isabel and her family and my daughter Claire. Occasionally my Mum comes too. My dog, Honey, used to be an integral part of these holidays and she along with Meg, my sister Isabel's dog, added immensely to the enjoyment of the walks in the Southern Upland hills and forests. Any dog lover will appreciate the delight of seeing their animal exploring new territory whilst waiting for their decrepit owner to catch up.

During this year's trip to Ashkirk I spent one day with Isabel's husband, my brother-in-law Stuart, walking in the Eildon hills close to Melrose. We started our walk (more like a squelch than a walk as it had rained and snowed heavily during the previous two weeks) at Newstead and parked next to a plaque that mentioned that this was the site of one of the largest Roman forts in Scotland (called Trimontium after the nearby three Eildon hills). Quite by accident we had parked alongside an old Roman fort. I assured Stuart that I had not chosen this walk because of the links to the Romans; it was mere coincidence. I am not too sure he believed me.

With all this talk of Scotland I sense another plan germinating; start at York, go via Carlisle, walk the length of that blasted Hadrian's Wall, and journey through Scotland, over the site of the Antonine Wall, to the outer limits that any Roman army ventured. And that answers the question of where to end – end where the Romans did, in the far north of Scotland at the Moray Firth. Again, Margary will be my constant companion. For purely scientific research purposes I would have to include a number of whisky distilleries along the way.

With regards to the reader searching out a Roman road and walking along its route, if only for a few yards, perhaps I should leave the final words in my book to Margary (page 7),

> *"But I hope your visiting will prove pleasant and informing, for these roads vary in character like individuals; some are frank and disclose their features readily, others are very shy and retiring, whilst some are downright unapproachable. A good specimen striding across the land is, however, a fine sight well worth a visit."*

REFERENCES AND OTHER BACKGROUND READING

Alcock, Joan. *Life in Roman Britain*. B.T. Batsford 1996.

Allason-Jones, L. *Women in Roman Britain, New Edition*. Council for British Archaeology 2005.

BBC Religion. *http://www.bbc.co.uk/religion/religions/christianity/history/uk_1.shtml* 2014.

Bidwell, Paul. *Roman Forts in Britain*. B.T. Batsford 1997.

Bishop M.C. *The Secret History of the Roman Roads of Britain*, Pen and Sword Military 2014.

Boardman, John et al. *The Oxford History of the Classical World*. Oxford University Press 1986.

Britainexpress.com. *http://www.britainexpress.com/History/english-parish-churches.htm.*

Britannia History. *http://www.britannia.com/history/bb51.html* 2007.

Caesar, Julius. *Gallic War*. Loeb.

Cornell, Tim and Matthews, John. *Atlas of the Roman World*. Phaidon Press 1982.

Churchill, Winston. *The Island Race*. Webb and Bower 1985.

Cunliffe, Barry. *Britain Begins*. Oxford University Press 2013.

Davies, Hugh. *Roman Roads in Britain*. Shire 2008.

Dio, Cassius. *Roman History, Books 56-60*. Harvard University Press 1924.

Dio, Cassius. *Roman History, Books 61-70*. Harvard University Press 1925.

Frere, S. *Britannia, a History of Roman Britain*. Routledge and Kegan Paul 1987.

Gascoigne, Bamber. *"History of Communication" Historyworld. From 2001 ongoing. http://www.historyworld.net/wrldhis/PlainTextHistories.asp?grou pid=1457&HistoryID=aa93&gtrack=pthc*

Heritagedaily.com. *https://www.heritagedaily.com/2013/03/in-the-footsteps-of-the-missing-ninth-legion-hispana-part-one/78078*

Higgins, Charlotte. *Under Another Sky, Journeys in Roman Britain*. Jonathan Cape 2013.

Hinde, Thomas. *The Domesday Book*. Book Club Associates 1985.

Historical Roman Britain. *Historical Map Guide (Folded Map)*. Ordnance Survey 2016.

Innis, Harold. *Empire and Communications*. Dundurn Press 2007.

Johnston, David. *An Illustrated History of Roman Roads in Britain*. Spurbooks 1979.

Jones, Barri and Mattingly, David. *An Atlas of Roman Britain*. Oxbow Books 2007.

Livingston, Helen. *In the Footsteps of Caesar: Walking Roman Roads in Britain*. Dial House 1995.

Livingston, Helen. *Kent – Pictorial Memories.* Waterton Press 1998.

Lord, Derek. *http://www.open-sandwich.co.uk/town_history/richborough_port.htm* . 2003

Margary, Ivan D. *Roman Roads in Britain*. J. Baker 1973.

Mattingly, David. *An Imperial Possession, Britain in the Roman Empire*. Allen Lane 2006.

Millett, Martin. *Roman Britain*. B.T. Batsford 1997.

Peel, J.H.B. *Along the Roman Roads of Britain*. Littlehampton 1971.

Plumbingsupply.com. https://www.plumbingsupply.com/pmroman.html. 1986

Postgate, Oliver. *Becket – An Illumination of the Life and Death of Thomas Becket*. Kingfisher 1989.

Ross, David. *England, History of a Nation*. Geddes and Grosset 2005.

Roth, Jonathan. *The Logistics of the Roman Army at War (264BC-AD235)*. Brill 1999.

Salway, Peter. *The Oxford Illustrated History of Roman Britain*. Oxford University Press 1993.

Southern, Patricia. *Roman Britain, a New History 55BC – AD 450*. Amberley 2011.

Tacitus. *The Annals, the Reigns of Tiberius, Claudius and Nero*. Oxford University Press 2008.

Welch, George. *Britannia, the Roman Conquest and Occupation of Britain*. Wesleyan 1963.

Wilkinson, Philip. *What the Romans Did for Us*. Boxtree 2000.

ACKNOWLEDGMENTS

Phil Sturgess for his tireless reading of the manuscript and pointing out the many amendments that needed making.

Createspace self-publishing for helping turn a dream into reality.

My parents who helped to instil in me a thirst for knowledge and for always supporting me.

I have been unable to trace the copyright owner of Ivan Margary's *"Roman Roads in Britain".*

Interrogation of the European Union Intellectual Property Office indicates that in file number 821 2801 the work titled "Roman Roads in Britain", published by John Baker 1973, has been recorded as an Orphan Work.

On that basis I have included the quotes from Margary's book.

I gratefully acknowledge the following kind permission given by, or on behalf of, the originators of quotes used in this book:

Professor Lindsay Allason-Jones gave permission for the use of quotes from her book *"Women in Roman Britain, New Edition".*

My namesake, David Ross, gave permission for quotes from the *"Britainexpress"* website.

The texts quoted from Patricia Southern's *"Roman Britain, a New History 55BC – AD 450"* were reproduced with kind permission of Amberley Publishing.

Bob and Sue Fielder allowed me to use quotes by the late Derek Lord from the *"open-sandwich"* website.

Permission to use quotes from Phillip Wilkinson's *"What the Romans Did for Us"* was given via the web tool "PLSclear".

DIO CASSIUS, VOL. VIII, translated by Earnest Cary, Loeb Classical Library Volume 176, Cambridge, Mass.: Harvard University Press, First published 1925. Loeb Classical Library ® is a registered trademark of the President and Fellows of Harvard College.

Permission to use a quote from the BBC Religion website was granted by Vicky Mitchell, Business Affairs Executive.

Permission to use quotes from *"The Logistics of the Roman Army at War (264BC-AD235)"* was given by the author, Professor Jonathan Roth.

Ben Kennedy, Permissions Team Lead at OUP kindly granted permission to use quotes from Tacitus, *"The Annals, the Reigns of Tiberius, Claudius and Nero"* and Salway, Peter, *"The Oxford Illustrated History of Roman Britain"*.

I include the following sources under the "Fair Use" principle:

Frere, S. *"Britannia, a History of Roman Britain"*.

Gascoigne,Bamber. *"History of Communication"*.

Printed in Great Britain
by Amazon